ADDITIONAL PRAISE

"Quist's precise composition illustrates the complexities of Black experiences in America in their sincerest forms—as greater cosmologies—birthed from the combustion of searing tongues and alchemic thoughts that allow us our rightful infinities. What was bounded is now boundless."

—Ron Austin, author of
Avery Colt Is a Snake, a Thief, a Liar

"I feel like *To Those Bounded* really gives a damn about me because it articulates the overwhelming impossibility of growing up Black: the ways this country tells us we are simultaneously 'too much' and 'inadequate,' and how we have to constantly fight those impossible limitations instead of nurturing the full spectrum of our humanity. And I'm serious as hell when I say that every teacher, professor, police, social worker, etc. should read this book, as well as every Black person who wants/needs a little more care, understanding, and tenderness."

Steven Dunn, author of
Water & Power

TO THOSE BOUNDED

To Those Bounded

© 2021 Donald Edem Quist

Published by Awst Press
P.O. Box 49163
Austin, TX 78765

awst-press.com
awst@awst-press.org

Printed in the United States of America
Distributed by Small Press Distribution

ISBN: 978-1-7367659-2-0

Library of Congress Control Number: 2021942073

Cover illustration by Maggie Chiang
Editing by Tatiana Ryckman
Copyediting by Emily Roberts
Book design by LK James

In Memory of
Edward Ruffin & Rev. John Foster III

CONTENTS

"Limited as we are in every way, this state which holds the mean between two extremes is present in all our impotence."

—Blaise Pascal (*Pensées*, 72)

"I was discussing the difficulties, the obstacles, the very real danger of death thrown up by the society when a Negro, when a Black man, attempts to become a man."

—James Baldwin (*The Dick Cavett Show*, 1968)

TO THOSE BOUNDED

DONALD EDEM QUIST

Run; until the skin sweats blood, keep going, until the heart dries out, move, until your weary muscles flake apart and the bones in your limbs splinter and crack.

Then go on.

Because, although they've always stalked you, you hear them behind you now.

Push harder.

Ignore the leaves and branches crunching under the feet of your pursuer. Run; until the trees and foliage blur green. Do not turn to follow the sounds of your peers splashing through the creek to avoid capture, the sounds of friends dropping cases of beer and the frenzied rustling through the forest shrubbery to hide themselves.

Do not stop to fret for your fellow minors.

You must escape.

Because history proves arrest could have different, more violent results for you.

Your detention would last long after your release.

Dismiss the idea, the inevitability of your imprisonment and that something inherent about you needs to be confined.

Speed up. Go farther.

Don't falter. Don't trip.

Run.

Be quicker, faster. Strive harder.

Find new stamina. Never rest.

Be better.

Or you'll be gone.

1. THIEVES

Whenever news outlets report the killing of a young African American male suspected of stealing, I remember how Chris Grayson taught me to shoplift. He taught me to make liters of soda vanish into puffy knockoff North Face jackets, to walk without crunching potato chip bags squeezed against my belly, to tuck bottom cuffs into Timberland boots and slide packs of candy-coated chocolate down my pant legs. I can't recall how we'd started stealing, but every weekday, when the bus dropped us at our apartment complex after school, Chris and I would walk into the nearby Safeway and walk out a few minutes later with a bundle of pilfered goods.

Sometimes we'd go in with a strategy. Chris would have a list of items he wanted: instant noodles, toilet paper, soap, stuff a little more challenging because we had to think up clever ways to free them from bulk packaging. I welcomed the difficulty because I enjoyed planning. Crouched behind a dumpster of rotten produce, I'd sketch a map of the supermarket aisles on wide-rule notebook paper so we could scheme. This always impressed Chris. I was the weakest student in my fourth-grade class and the teacher often reprimanded me—but Chris called me smart. Other students at our elementary school teased me about my weight—but Chris considered my size an asset. I could conceal more junk in my larger clothes. He appreciated these things. He also noticed that the employees at the Safeway tended to pay more attention to me than to him. We used this to our advantage. I'd linger near a stock boy while Chris snuck items past the employee's peripheral vision.

I liked when Chris complimented me. I felt helpful when we succeeded in taking the stuff he said he needed. Whenever we dared each other to grab as much as we could, Chris was never upset that I always managed to get the most. Retreating with our booty to the dimly lit, piss-reeking stairwells of our neighborhood, we'd divide the spoils. We'd congratulate each other on a job well done, and Chris would thank me before cramming snacks into his mouth.

x

I'd only visited his apartment once. Walking past a trash-collection area in our neighborhood, Chris had spotted a round end table leaning against one of the communal dumpsters. It had significant scuffs and scratches, but it stood straight, and we both thought the nautical compass decal on the top looked cool. He said he wanted to use it as a nightstand and asked if I could carry it to his mom's place.

Chris led the way to the apartment. His building stood at the very end of the line of four-story concrete units that composed our housing development. I was shocked how much his home resembled mine, only without the matching earth-toned furniture and my father's Ghanaian art. It was a bizarro-world version where nothing matched. In place of the scent of peppers, cocoa butter, and ant spray, Chris' apartment reeked of sweaty clothes and a stale sourness that I'd catch a whiff of whenever he shook his blond mop-top from his eyes.

He directed me to his bedroom, and I set the table beside a bare mattress on the floor. Then he asked if I'd like a pudding cup.

He had no clean utensils, so as we stood in the narrow galley-style kitchen, he instructed me on how to twist the aluminum seal of a Snack Pack into a spoon. Savoring lid-fulls of gooey chocolate, I asked when he expected his parents back. He shrugged, looking into his cup. Our afternoons together ended with me rushing home before my father or stepmother returned from work to discover me missing, but Chris was never in a hurry to get home.

Suddenly, I wanted to leave. I scrapped the last remnants of pudding and then asked Chris what else he thought we might find in the dumpsters. His eyes widened with excitement.

At the trash area again, he peered into one of the dumpsters through an open hatch. Fall breezes cleared away most of the odor emanating from the rubbish. Chris decided to investigate further. He dropped inside and began rummaging. I asked if he could see anything interesting, and he told me to come in and look for myself. I did, and after rooting through the trash bags for several minutes I picked out a cylinder-shaped appliance as long as my forearm.

I asked Chris what he thought.

He frowned and suggested I keep it if I thought it might have value.

I took the cylinder home to my dad's apartment.

The appliance oozed a white sludge the consistency of creamed wheat. I left the contraption in the bathtub to show my father. When he and my stepmom came home that evening, I presented it to him. Tired from a full day of chauffeuring lobbyists and politicos around D.C. in his taxi, my father glared at the appliance with what I'd later recognize as a rage born from bigger frustrations. He grabbed the device. He carried it through the apartment to the balcony and launched it over the railing. I watched the cylinder fly toward a grassy area below, then explode against the ground into chunks of metal, plastic, and foul porridge. Dad asked where I had discovered a broken garbage disposal and why I had brought it into his home. I described diving through the dumpster. I told him I thought the part might have some use.

Dad asked if Chris was with me. The small, dirty white boy, he said.

I nodded, surprised that my father knew anything about my friend. Dad told me never to go digging through the trash again. He demanded I take a shower and forbade me from speaking to Chris.

He would lead me into trouble I could not afford, Dad said. Chris and I were not the same.

Chris and I returned to the dumpsters after school the next day. Among the waste, Chris found a pair of worn-through moccasins. He assured me he could salvage them; we'd just have to run to the Safeway and steal duct tape to plug the soles. And maybe snatch a couple candy bars for later.

For months, Chris and I pillaged. We grew more brazen with every successful grab. Spring brought new challenges. Our winter clothes got packed away and our pants got shorter. With fewer layers to hide things, the risk of getting caught increased and so did the excitement. My grades fell as I spent more time running around with Chris than doing homework. He showed me how to forge my mom's signature on weekly progress reports. He had a lot of practice signing his own mother's name.

We carried on, devising inventive ways to smuggle goods from the supermarket. Our highlight: a maneuver that allowed Chris to escape with two twenty-ounce bottles of shampoo while wearing only a T-shirt, sandals, and a pair of jean shorts without underwear. Chris and I may have kept stealing until we ran into failure, but my father intervened.

The school had an in-service day. Our bus delivered us to our apartment complex by noon. We had twice as many hours as usual before my parents would come home. We decided to go to the grocery store, filch a bunch of junk food, and hang out at the local playground.

Entering the Safeway, I left my bookbag by the automatic doors. Chris never carried a backpack, not even to school. However, he thought to advise me that taking my bag into stores would arouse more suspicion.

We separated at Fresh Fruits and Vegetables. He continued straight through Meat and Poultry. I hooked left past Cereal, Pasta, then curved right between rows of cookies and crackers. I pocketed some Oreos and kept moving, making a U-turn onto Chips and Soft Drinks to meet Chris and snag some Mountain Dew.

At the end of the aisle hung a thin corner display for keychains. I hesitated over one of them. At the center of the coin-shaped trinket, the flat profile of a sea vessel spun on a tiny vertical bar. The bow and sails pointed right or left, starboard or port, changing direction depending on how I rotated the ship. I grabbed the keychain to inspect further. Chris nudged me to hurry. Holding items for too long, examining them too closely, could get us caught. I motioned to return the object with one hand but actually tucked the keychain into my pocket, pretending to search for a wallet. Chris once told me that looking confounded would convince onlookers we'd misplaced our money and had intentions of paying.

We hurried to the exit, miming forgetfulness.

I picked up my bag at the door and we walked out quietly, rounding the side of the building and rushing behind the loading dock.

A hill separated the shopping plaza and our apartment parking lot. On the far side of it, squatting in a space reserved for disabled drivers, we removed the snacks from our clothes and Chris began eating. I ripped the barcode from the key ring.

"Your dad?" Chris said.

Yes, I thought, the keychain did remind me of my father. Maybe my brain associated the encircled boat with Dad's immigration to America, crossing the Atlantic in search of better, and how his spirit was that of a landlocked traveler who yearned to voyage boundlessly. I thought how the keychain would look dangling from the ignition of his taxi. He might appreciate the gift.

"Your dad!" Chris repeated.

I looked up to see my father in his cab, rolling horizontally over the yellow lines painted on the asphalt. The passenger-side windows descended, and Dad ordered me into the car and shouted at Chris to go home. I murmured goodbye as I slid into the front seat with my head down. My father reached over, digging his fingers into my left arm. I flinched, waiting for his free hand to slap or knock me. But his other hand remained on the wheel as he asked where Chris and I had found the money to buy food.

I shrugged, wincing, and he tightened his grip.

Dad noticed the glittering item in my fist.

"What is that?"

I opened my hand. Dad snatched the keychain away. "Where did you get this?"

"It's for you," I said.

He sighed. He spun the ship and stared forward through the windshield. I squirmed, rubbing my thumbs along the outer seams of my shorts. When his gaze finally returned to me, his eyes were glistening.

"You and Chris are different," he said. His tone made his voice sound like a whisper. "You need to be more careful." Theft carried greater consequences for me than for Chris, he said, because our skin tones were different. My actions could even be used to stereotype others and make life harder for people who look like me.

I told him I didn't understand. I felt afraid of whatever

was causing the dampness in his eyes, the terrible thing behind his anger.

"*They* will paint boys like you with a broad brush," Dad said.

Perhaps my dad was familiar with W. E. B. Du Bois' insight that boys like me are made to possess a double-consciousness, to always be thinking how others perceive their actions. In the 1960s, Du Bois expatriated from the United States and moved his family to Accra, my dad's birthplace. But maybe my father had seen it for himself: The same laws that assured my friend due process might not extend to me because of the melanin in my skin.

Years later, I have access to endless information that forces me to understand the desperation in my father's eyes that day. I can bookmark, share, post, and tweet countless examples of young men brutalized or murdered under suspicion of stealing. I read about William Chapman: shot in the face and chest after being accused of stealing from a Walmart. And Tamon Robinson: run over by a patrol car as cops pursued him for stealing paving stones. And Kajieme Powell: killed by police responding to a 911 call about the theft of pastries and energy drinks. And

Arthur Adams: shot and killed after an employee accused him of stealing diapers.

On a video beneath the tagline "New Footage Raises Questions," a closed-circuit camera shows a boy swaying into Ferguson Market & Liquor at 0:12. He wears an oversized T-shirt, a red cap, khaki shorts with socks and sandals. A friend follows him, a shorter, thinner kid with locks. The angle shifts. At 0:32, the boy stands with his hands tucked behind his back. He stares patiently across the counter at the store attendant, whose face is blocked from our view by lottery ticket displays. The boy's companion paces at the end of one of the cramped aisles. 0:45, the boy reaches over the counter to collect a box of Swisher Sweets and turns to pass the cigarillos to his friend. The boy reaches his arm past the kiosk again at 0:57, faster this time, farther, and pulls back a larger box of cigars. The boy moves closer to the cash register, addressing the still-unseen store attendant. The friend places the box of Swishers on the counter. 1:07, while the friend eyes the exit and ambles toward the door, the boy bends to collect items that fell to the floor when he snatched the bigger box from over the counter. The boy slides to his left to a give a woman and her child room to pass as they enter the store at 1:13. The store attendant, an old man, materializes from behind the counter, rushing through the gap between the boy and the lady with her child. The angle shifts. The attendant moves to block the boy from leaving by standing in the doorway. But the boy is bigger, stronger, and at 1:29 the boy shoves the old man to the right. He bounces off a snack display, but nothing topples. At 1:31, the attendant grabs the boy's shirt to hold him still. The boy yanks his right arm free and steps toward the worker. The old man guards himself, lowering his head and raising his shoulder, twisting his torso away from the boy's potential blows. But the boy, with his chest swollen and arms held wide at his side, doesn't touch the old man again, and at 1:34, the boy spins on his left foot to hurry out the door after his smaller friend.

I watch the video a dozen more times.

Only one new question is raised for me and it is about the intent of the Ferguson Police Department—its decision to release this surveillance footage during a press conference emphasizing that the boy was suspected of stealing a box of cigars valued at $48.99. I wonder if the officers believed sharing this video would help those who identify with the boy—like me—to submit to his killing. To our own.

That last time I shoplifted with Chris Grayson, my father must have suspected I'd take advantage of the hours granted by the school's half day. His intervention stopped me from going to the supermarket with Chris again. But before Chris and I stopped speaking to each other, I attempted to describe to him, with not much success, how it had felt to watch my dad hurl the keychain out the driver's-side window. I'd tried to keep my eye on the trinket as it sailed through the air, but in spite of my desire that spinning boat vanished. I knew I couldn't continue to shoplift with Chris. But I still wondered what would happen to him. I think about where he is now and what he had to do to get by and how severely he was punished for it.

I hope, at least, one day he knows something other than scarcity.

2.

Every day.

3.

I heard them call my father illegal, alien.

He came from a gold-speckled coast as something other.

I'm sitting at a desk, alone in a classroom smaller than any other classroom in my middle school. Every half hour, a teacher or the school resource officer enters to make sure I'm doing the math work I need to complete so I'm not a child left behind. I'm in the eighth grade, and I'm on the verge of staying in the eighth grade for another year. I've missed a lot of class because of suspensions, because I keep getting in fights with other students and verbal altercations with my teachers. Like how I called one of the media center librarians "a despicable bourgeois asshole" for belly-laughing when I asked if the school had a copy of *The Communist Manifesto* by Engels and Marx, and like the time I hooked my fingers behind the front teeth of a boy who stole my chocolate milk and dragged him several feet by his blood-drooling mouth. Out-of-school suspension hasn't done much for correcting my bursts of anger. I've received so many weeks away that the vice principal thought to confine me to in-school suspension. So now I'm sitting in this mini classroom. I come to this room in the morning and don't leave until the busses arrive at the end of the day. I'm escorted to the bathroom if I need to go, and lunch is brought to me from the cafeteria on a tray. I sit quietly, no talking, nothing to do but count the clicks of the wall clock and complete the assignments provided by my teachers. I'm doing the work. I don't want to return to middle school next year. I want to go on to high school. Last week the vice principal told my mom and me that the school had reached out to county administrators and recommended me for expulsion from the school district. The vice principal used the word *dangerous* a lot. Part of me liked that, but another part didn't. What made me dangerous? I never start it. Someone else always laughs at how I dress or look or act or smell. They call me an Oreo or say I'm trying to be white, and I get mad. The vice principal said my size makes a difference. I'm bigger than most every other student and large enough to intimidate some of the teachers. The last time my mom was called to the school to pick me up for fighting, she refused. She said she was tired of it. *It* being me, I guess. My dad had to come get me. As he escorted me out of the front office, threatening under his breath to whip me with his belt as soon as he got me back to his apartment, we were stopped at the front entrance of the building by the vice principal. She spoke to my father like she was a family friend or an auntie. She said she didn't mean to assume, but my behavior suggested I probably could use more discipline at home. My dad's brow furrowed and his eyes turned to lasers he might have wished to shoot through her. She said, "Our children need to act better, Mr. Quist. They can't just behave the same way some of these other students do. You understand?" My dad said he did understand, and we shuffled quietly to his taxi to head to his place and wait until my mom could pick me up after work. At his apartment, I braced myself for blows from his heavy palms and raps from his knuckles and belt buckle. But they never came. He sat with me in the living room for a bit. He studied me while I chewed the skin around my fingernails and tried to avoid eye contact. He asked, "Why do you keep getting into trouble?" I said, "I don't know. I just feel angry all the time." He nodded like he understood. "It's hard to be good all the time," he said. Sitting here in in-school suspension, I'm thinking about that. I'm thinking about the vice principal's words and how my dangerousness means I have to miss out on the end-of-the-year school trip to Adventure World amusement park. I'm trying to force myself to focus on quadratic equations and graphing functions, but the slopes and rises just remind me of the rollercoasters all the other eighth graders are riding elsewhere. I flip my calculator upside-down and I try to make words: 58008, BOOBS, 7734, hELL, and 35007, LOOSE. I try for the longest word I can with the keypad—55,373,604—it looks like hOPELESS. I scan the room and every empty desk around me. I lean back in my own seat and my glance slides up to the ceiling, and then eventually back down to the math paper in front of me. I've struggled with algebra and geometry. I strain to understand why I would ever need to solve for x, or how that hidden value could have a single answer. My math teacher had recently talked about these things called bounded functions. How, when put on a graph, these functions have limits that prevent them from going too far one way or another. But I don't understand. I asked my teacher who sets the limits. The teacher said it depends. On what? The needs of the desired functions. I'm stuck in a giant 3-D graph that fills the room. On the graph a dark coaster car bounces between parallel dotted lines that never intersect. There is no rest. I get dizzy from darting between limits, up and down, up and down, forever.

5.

Every day, consider every piece of clothing to ensure a non-threatening appearance.

6. DELINQUENT

Two weeks after I turned sixteen, days before Thanksgiving, I broke into a friend's house. I didn't do it alone. We smashed the basement window to get in. We called the cable company to order pay-per-view porn, pocketed objects to pawn, and tried to drink everything in the family liquor cabinet, filling the empty bottles with tap water.

My friend came home sooner than expected.

He called the police.

I ran away.

When I arrived at my own house, I found an officer waiting for me, detailing the crime to my mother. After the officer left, my mother screamed, pleading to know *why*. I had no definitive answer. I told her I wasn't alone. She shook her head and reminded me that I didn't look like my fellow culprits, that the consequences would be different for me.

My mother grieved through the holiday. For days she cried, sometimes breaking into tears when we'd make eye contact. Each night her howling sobs and wails kept me awake. On one of those evenings, she floated into my room, and I pretended to be asleep. I listened to her pray over me softly. The law frightened her in a way I hadn't learned yet. I listened to her quiet pleas. She feared she had failed to impart to me some crucial lesson about how to stay alive. My mother feared I was some precious thing, about to vanish.

The following day, I went to my friend's house to apologize to him and his family. I gave them all the money I had in my savings account. I offered to help resolve the collective damages. When I came home, I apologized to my mother.

After Thanksgiving break, the same officer returned. He told my mom and I that my friend's family would not pursue criminal charges. The county police department would no longer investigate the crime. My delinquency had been forgiven.

I felt as relieved for my mother as for myself.

But the cop's parting words undercut my relief. Before turning to leave, he addressed me directly to say he'd encouraged my friend's family to pursue legal action, but they hadn't listened. If it'd been up to him, he would have arrested me. And if he ever caught me again, he said, he'd make sure I'd be punished.

As I watched him exit, I wondered if he had said the same thing to the other perpetrators. I didn't do it alone. Did the cop mean to say *you all* instead of only *you*? Did the officer convey to the others—the kids with lighter skin—that he'd be waiting for them, too?

[7.]

"I lock your persona in a dream-inducing sleeper hold

    While your better selves watch from the bleachers."

My mother appears in the doorway of my bedroom. She has to raise her voice over the clamoring of Jimmy Eat World. I glance up at her, but I'm not prepared to reduce the volume. Sitting cross-legged on the floor, I have the liner notes from *Bleed American* open on my lap. I've resolved to memorize all the words to "A Praise Chorus."

My mother lingers. I concede and lean toward the large six-disc CD player that fills the lowest shelf of my bookcase. I turn the dial left and ask her to repeat herself.

She says a name I don't recognize and I ask, "What about him?"

She wonders if I know him; he goes to my high school.

As the band hits the bridge, my favorite part, *crimson and clover, over and over*, I offer my mother an inflated sigh to convey how annoyed I am by this intrusion.

"He died," she says, "this afternoon in a car crash on Midcounty Highway. He was sixteen."

I look down at the lyrics printed in the thick matte pamphlet.

I respond, "Okay?"

My mother says she'll pray for him. She exits, shuffling to another part of the house.

I try to return to the music. I raise the volume again. But the name my mother mentioned echoes over the chorus of "Your House."

On the shelf above the CD player, I see my high school yearbooks. I reach for the most recent one and pull it down. I use the index to search for the name. The page number leads me to a familiar face.

"Doobie," escapes my lips, barely audible. I flip back to the index and search desperately for an alternative, other names my mother might have mispronounced, and other names I might have misheard. Gradually the realization covers me. Doobie has died.

The album arrives at track six, "Hear You Me." I've never noticed the significant shift in tempo. This song feels more introspective and sobering, an antithesis to the cathartic speed of the album's opening title or the rebellious frenzy of "Sweetness," a foil to the empowering optimism and deceptively childlike rhythms of "The Middle." As lead vocalist and guitarist Jim

Adkins croons of an untimely death, memories of Doobie confront me.

I must have seen him earlier today. I must have nodded to him as we passed in the hall.

I can't consider him a close friend. We hang out only occasionally. We have mutual acquaintances. His sister and I both play in the marching band. But Doobie being a sophomore, and I a senior, we don't share any classes or see each other much in school.

Wait...

No. Past tense.

We used to have mutual acquaintances.

We used to hang out occasionally.

The most time I ever spent talking to Doobie was a few weeks ago. He had approached me before school to buy some weed. Smiling, I asked him why he assumed I could get him drugs. He chuckled, pretended to sniff me, and then pointed to my red eyes.

I had never sold drugs before, but the prospect excited me. The following day I handed Doobie an eighth of marijuana and he gave me $60. Most of the money would go to my friend who had covered the purchase from our regular dealer in Germantown. I didn't need the cash, but it was welcomed, and I reveled in the opportunity to appear cool to Doobie.

My mother discovered the money rummaging through my dresser drawers for toenail clippers. She asked why I was hiding cash. I told her I wasn't. She asked where the dollar bills had come from, and I offered a lame excuse about withdrawing money from my bank account to buy a used video game from a friend. I thought this lie had believability, and I still had funds saved from working seasonal hours at KB Toys the previous fall.

But my mother seemed skeptical. She shook her head solemnly and told me to be careful. "You got to do better, Donnie," she said.

Was Doobie high when he died? Am I somehow partly responsible in his loss?

The album has reached the eerie industrial introduction to "Get It Faster." Faint scratches and sounds like clanging, drippy factory pipes lead to an explosion of percussion and crunchy power chords. But this isn't what I'm looking for right now. I want to continue the contemplations with less aggression and more angst. I close the yearbook and return it to the shelf. I hit the arrows pointing right to skip forward.

Through the album's final act.

I settle on the last song, "My Sundown."

I close my eyes and lie back onto the carpet.

Growing feedback and ambient noise like a vinyl record pulled in reverse gives way to the lull of Adkins' stanzas and quick, gentle strums on an acoustic guitar. The song builds, adding layers—finger snaps, fast taps on the hi-hats. Then, Rachel Haden's wispy vocals reinforce Adkins', followed by a second layer of her feminine lilt—and then a brief memory, hazy from malt liquor and thick pot smoke. I was at a small party in the basement of Doobie's parents' house. Doobie and I shared a blunt while a girl massaged his scalp. I sat coughing. Entranced, I watched the girl's thin digits twirl the greasy thatch atop Doobie's skull. I can't remember what Doobie and I chatted about, or if we spoke at all, but I enjoyed his company. I will miss him.

The bars are suddenly stripped of their layers, torn down again to their sparse foundation.

No one cares, Adkins says. *No one cares*.

Other memories pile on. All the times *I* should have met my end. When I skipped school and broke into a friend's house and his parents threatened to press charges; when police discovered narcotics in the trunk of the limo I joined to junior prom; when I was nearly arrested for underage drinking during the senior homecoming dance, but the two friends detained by law enforcement didn't give my name; when I nearly flipped my mother's Ford Explorer racing someone on Montgomery Village Avenue.

Every instance should have been an end.

But things rise again during the second verse, reconstructing now-familiar layers even stronger than before. Beneath the steady drumming and the simple bass and snare—*boom-bap-boom-boom-bap*—driving to a single cymbal crash and chopstick-pokes to the keys of a piano.

Now, fully actualized, the voices evolve into conversation, a call and response:

I want to be so much more than this, says Haden.

No one cares, Adkins responds.

"Is there any point in trying for better?" I ask no one.

Over and over again, until the drums vanish with most of

34

the orchestration, an abrupt dive and then a gradual floating upwards, through the sprawling studio effects expanding infinitely like space.

Today is not forever, I think.

"I could be so much more than this."

Years from now I'll remember crying for Doobie as I sang along softly.

Good good bye.

I'll be fine.

Good good bye.

Good good night.

9.

Every day, avoid gathering outside with friends unless the majority of the group is white.

[10.]

"...there was usually some part of me guaranteed to offend everybody's comfortable prejudices of who I should be. That is how I learned that if I didn't define myself for myself, I would be crunched into other people's fantasies for me and eaten alive."

I hear someone shout "Riot," and I'm not sure if it is an observation or a command. I ignore it. I'm shuffling across the quad toward the student residence halls with Roshida and Heather. Roshida and I act as crutches for Heather, who sags between us. One of my arms wraps around Heather's waist as her head hangs low, mumbling to herself. She's drunk and nearly passed out. The hinge of her left elbow has hooked my neck, and although it's almost 2 a.m. on a cool spring night, I'm sweating heavily from the effort. On the other side of Heather's body, Roshida doesn't seem as stressed from dragging our friend as I am. Roshida's smiling and cracking jokes that neither she nor Heather will remember the next day. I'm sober. I was designated to drive us back from a former truck stop renovated into a large Mexican restaurant and bar, El Rancho. They don't card at El Rancho; half the population of our small South Carolinian liberal arts college was there tonight, guzzling too-cheap, too-strong margaritas and grinding on each other to Dancehall-inspired songs featuring Sean Paul. Heather is small. She's a dance major, living on PB&J sandwiches and the microwavable mac-and-cheese packets I keep in my dorm room. There isn't enough in her to slow the alcohol shutting her down, and with every step I can feel her becoming dead weight.

I tell Roshida, "We might have to carry her."

Roshida laughs harder. She jokes about how two people with our skin would look carrying a pale, unconscious Heather by her arms and legs through the dark.

"Someone would call the cops, man," she cackles. "We'd be fucking shot!"

Imagining it, I can't help but laugh, too, in that sad way when something is especially funny because it is so fucked up and true.

"But we're RAs. People would recognize us."

Roshida tells me to hush. "Keep going; we're almost there."

I remind her there is no elevator to our floor, and Roshida groans.

Yards away someone shouts, "RIOT!" again, louder than before.

I ask Roshida what she thinks is going on. She tells me it's nothing. It must be nothing, because nothing happens here. Roshida and I have served as resident advisors since August and besides a few drinking violations and one of the sophomores on my hall sneaking a pitbull into her room, there's been nothing too crazy. Nothing like a riot.

"RIOT!"

"Maybe it is something," I say. "We should go check."

Roshida stops moving forward and I almost lose my hold on Heather.

"Homie, what do you want us to do, drag Heather all the way over there to see what's going on?"

Heather's skull bobs up and her eyes flutter open. She pumps her jaw, trying to relearn how to speak. "No," she manages to say, and then, "Don't go."

The three of us pause, our faces zebra-ed by the shadow of oak branches crowding outdoor security lighting. Under our silence, shouts rise on the opposite end of campus. I debate with Roshida, pausing between shrill screams carried on magnolia-scented air. Heather wobbles between us as I speak about our duty and responsibility.

"Nigga, we're just RAs. You're talking like we took an oath or something."

"Protecting other students is the job."

"You're being dumb."

Roshida twists her neck under Heather's arm and peers in the direction of the commotion. She sighs and pulls Heather closer. I let Heather slide off me and cling to Roshida. Both of them twist their faces in disapproval. Roshida doesn't bother telling me good luck. The pair stumble on without me.

I watch them for a bit before I turn to rush toward the shouting.

My body and legs feel lighter, and I lean into the urge to sprint.

Figures start to appear on the horizon in a courtyard adjoining two of the residence halls with the science building and a parking lot.

I don't find a riot, but a brawl. More than half a dozen shifting, writhing cells of violent human bodies. At the nuclei, young men pummel each other while onlookers circle them, chanting, cheering, and booing. At the center of each battle there are at least two fighters: one brown and one beige. I recognize them as members of the basketball and baseball teams.

During my interview for the resident advisor position, the

dean of student services asked me why I wanted the job. I had anticipated the question. I listed examples of my contributions to campus life: my freshman year on the Dean's List, my participation in student theater productions, years as a library work-study employee, volunteering for new student orientation events and resurrecting the school's literary magazine after years of inactivity, standing on the college president's blue-ribbon committee, and organizing open mic nights downtown. I explained how becoming an RA was a natural progression, another way to express my commitment to community-building and broadening diversity among student leadership.

I didn't mention that becoming an RA was also another way to prove myself to others. In the eyes of many of my white high school teachers, I was an underachiever not living up to the excellence of famed African American scholars and activists with whom they thought I shared some kind of resemblance. I seemed to get penalized for unrealized potential. I didn't realize until after graduation how much I was bothered by the subtle ways those teachers communicated their disappointment. When I managed to find a college that would accept me and my mediocre GPA, I committed myself to becoming someone those teachers would consider an exceptional student of color.

If my white college professors ever suggested I was a letdown, I'd know it wasn't because I hadn't tried hard enough.

Standing at the edge of the fight, I realize I've waited for a moment like this since I accepted the RA position: a chance to stand out as *good*.

I shove through the nearest crowd and throw my body between the fighters at the center. I succeed in pushing them apart, but not without a stray punch to my back. Only the adrenaline keeps me standing. Some of the onlookers reach out and hook the arms and waists of the brawlers. The basketball player struggles to wrestle himself free. He's screaming, "Say it again! Call me *nigger* again." The baseball player's eyes are spinning, wild, bulging and blue. He's wobbling in his peer's arms. The ripped collar of his deep V-neck shirt reveals patches of flush pink skin across his chest and a thin gold cross on a chain dangling from his red neck. The baseball player doesn't respond to the basketball player. He doesn't respond when I ask them both to explain what has happened. After a few seconds of heavy breathing, he runs, darting from the grips of the people trying to hold him, bursting through the crowd and pushing a girl to the ground. The guys who had tried to subdue the baseball player chase after him, and then so do I.

The baseball player bolts up a flight of steps leading from the courtyard to the entrance of one of the dormitories. A recycling roll-cart is on its side, propping open the doors of the residence hall. The baseball player hops the bin, his pursuers and I close behind. On the first floor, students have been drawn out of their rooms by the roars outside and the energy rising around them. The baseball player barrels past them as he widens the distance between him and me. I yell for everyone to return to the safety of their rooms. The baseball player and his athletic peers reach the stairwell at the end of the floor and rush up the stairs.

I'm not sure what I'll do if I catch up to them. I don't stop to consider my flip-phone bouncing in my pants pocket or calling the police. My experience has ingrained in me a distrust of law enforcement. Part of me understands there is a potential for police officers to make the racial disputes outside worse. I don't want anyone to be arrested or shot to death. I think maybe I can handle this myself.

On the second level, the baseball player zig-zags across the hall, trying to read the numbered room plates beside each door. His pursuers have reached his side now, trying to speak to him, telling him to *let it go*. One door and its numbers bring them all to a stop. I've almost caught up. I'm close enough to see the splats of blood on the baseball player's knuckles as he starts to pound the door with the bottoms of his tight fists. I want to prevent the baseball player from hurting anyone else. I want to help keep the peace. But I am struggling to contain an atomic anger. So much of my body wants to exorcise its rage onto the flesh of this baseball player and anyone who looks like him. When the door springs open, I'm close enough to see a face peek out that looks like a basketball player I've seen around campus. The baseball player kicks his way into the room, and his friends tumble in after him. The door slams shut and locks. I bang my flat-open palms against the door until my hands sting. I can hear the shouting and scuffle on the other side. I imagine a scene like the ones outside.

"RIOT!"

Maybe someone outside can tell me how this started and help me end it.

I race downstairs.

Arguments have broken out in the hallway of the first floor, no longer just baseball and basketball players. Running back to the courtyard, I find the cells have merged and grown. I can't spot a clear way to break the thrashing mass apart.

I start scanning for something I can climb to try to raise my voice above the crowd. A few feet away, I spot a shaking head, a foot taller than most others. It's a basketball player named Jackson. I speed over.

Jackson's teammates often tease him for being an Oreo and liking *white people shit*. People say the same kind of things about me. During my freshman year, Jackson and I met up a few times to play *Tony Hawk's Pro Skater* on PS2. Once, he and I hopped on a game of air hockey in the student union building. He beat me at both. Schooled me on Tony Hawk with his effortless grinds and trick combinations, and he could make the air puck slide too fast for my eyes to follow. But he wouldn't brag for too long after he'd won. Jackson was cool. We once spent an afternoon listening to *Stankonia* on his boombox and chatting about how much we admired the aesthetics of André 3000. We might have become friends, but Jackson spent most of his time with members of his team, many of whom I suspect think I'm uncool.

When I reach Jackson, I ask if he knows what started all the fighting tonight.

His sight stays focused on the crowd as he shrugs, "Dunno. One of ours danced with one of their girls at Rancho tonight and the team decided to start shit."

One of ours?

I ask, "Nobody tried to fight you?"

Jackson grins and shakes his head again, his eyes moving between the fights in front of us. "No, those boys know better and I know better." Jackson explains that he was born in South Carolina, grew up in this town where our college stands on grounds formerly farmed by slaves. He knew better, and maybe the boys on the baseball team knew Jackson's large family and circle of friends in the area could make their time in town difficult if they were to provoke him. "Some of my teammates, these dudes from the North, it's like they've never been called *nigger* before," Jackson says. "Me, I've been called worse by better people."

I ask him if he'll help me try to end all the fighting, and for the first time his eyes leave the brawl. He turns to look down at me and asks why.

I remind him people are getting hurt and that there will be consequences for his teammates.

Jackson laughs. "Ay, these people are going to fight. You and I can't stop them. Let them have it out." He looks back to the raging mob, cups both hands around his mouth and shouts,

"RIOT!" He folds his arms and chuckles to himself, but soon he is shaking his head again.

And suddenly I feel dumb for believing I might ever resolve a fight as big as racism. I don't know what to do. So I stand there next to Jackson, waiting for the battling cells to die out or multiply. We stand. Waiting. Watching. It's not a riot, but I sense one rising up my throat.

Soon more RAs arrive. A few of them have cell phones and take turns flipping up their screens and calling the police. When the cops arrive, students scatter and flee. Most run back into the dorms. A few of the baseball and basketball players are too slow to escape and get zip-tied and walked to the paddy wagon the officers have driven onto part of the courtyard. Jackson runs, too, perhaps instinctually. When the police question the other RAs and me about what happened, I notice the officer's eyes glide to my pale-skinned fellows for confirmation after everything I say. One of the cops looks me over, his gaze lingering on the rings of perspiration on my shirt. He asks if I'm sure I wasn't *involved* in the fight. I'm confused by the wording of the officer's question, but I say no.

On the walk to my own room, I've never heard the campus so quiet. The air is frozen. Nothing moves. Nothing breathes but me. The cool evening wheezes through my lungs. My tired bones shuffle and creak. My sneakers drag granules of sand and earth across sidewalk pavement, shushing the campus to sleep. In the morning there will be incident reports and repercussions, but for now there is a kind of false peace.

My room smells like tequila sweat.

Roshida has left Heather snoring in my bed. I stand over her body. Moonlight through the Venetian blinds frames her silhouette across my navy-blue comforter. I study Heather for a moment. Her long, honey-colored hair falls across her face. She's small. Even sprawled on her back with her arms stretched wide, she still seems tiny.

My relationship with Heather is complicated. We are friends but we've kissed and groped each other a few times when no one was around. Heather and I never have conversations about these intimacies, never discuss the reasons why we aren't dating, or why it feels like we both avoid displaying our affection in public. I'm sure some folks who see Heather and me together notice how we laugh and ways we look out for one another. They might wonder if we're having sex. But we aren't, and we aren't a couple, and the obstacles to us becoming more than friends seem bigger than just admitting our desires. The obstacles are cloudy and incalculable and rooted in histories much older than either of us. Because women like Heather can bring danger to men like me. Some part of me has always been vaguely aware of this, but now I start to consider how even our knowing each other can become treacherous. I wonder who might see her as she leaves my room after dawn, and if it would embolden the kind of rage I saw tonight.

Standing over Heather in the dark, watching her milk-skin reflect the moon's beams, I remember Sarah Page and Dick Rowland and massacres in Tulsa. I remember Rosewood, Florida. I remember Carolyn Bryant and Emmett Till's murder, and a hundred stories about lynchings and beatings, and at least one warning from my grandmother when I first started dating: *Be careful; they get crazy about their women.* I imagine the violent possibilities of this small prank Roshida has left in my bed, and I laugh a little laugh that kind of sounds like Jackson's, the sad chuckle of something especially funny because it is so fucked up and true.

12.

Every day, worry about being stopped by police. Every. Day.

[13.]

"Looks like a bad dude, too. Could be on something."

14.

Standing in front of Safeway, I wait for my rideshare to arrive. A few minutes after 11 p.m., a police cruiser speeds onto the curb in front of the grocery store, forcing me to step backward. I experience a moment of fear, assuming that I have done something wrong.

A pair of officers exits the cruiser and moves toward a boy wearing a white hoodie.

The boy has one hand pressing a cellphone to his head.

The boy has a skateboard cradled in his other arm.

He's a few feet diagonal from me, and I notice one of the officers approach the boy from behind. The cops surround the boy, reaching, grabbing, and patting his pockets and body. The young man stares out, calm, still on the phone, as authorities search him.

I overhear an officer ask the boy why he is "walking around."

I'm prompted to consider how moving through a public space or standing in front of a grocery store is inherently suspicious.

My rideshare driver arrives—his name is Manny, according

to my smartphone application. But he continues to roll past the front of the store and around to the side of the supermarket. I jog after my ride. I leave the boy alone with the officers.

I find Manny parked in front of an Indian grocery store. He lowers his windows and shouts that it is okay to get in. When I enter the car, Manny laughs and says, "When I saw the cops, I thought they were for you." He offers this as an explanation as to why he didn't stop the car to collect me from the designated location. I say to Manny, "They could've been." On the ride to my destination, I ask Manny to tell me about himself. Manny's from El Salvador. He's lived in America for ten years. Manny's studying for the GRE and GMAT to pursue an MBA at East Bay. I listen and then ask more questions. I chat idly, sharing a little about my experience living abroad in Asia.

But my thoughts never stray too far from the boy.

I hope he made it home safely.

I hope he forgives me for leaving.

15.

I'm a big fan of syndicated reality TV courtroom shows—
Judge Judy, *The People's Court*, and *Judge Faith* are among my
absolute favorites. I started watching them as a child, during
too-hot-to-play-outside summer afternoons at my maternal
grandmother's home. Tucked beside her on a ratty loveseat,
I watched her chain-smoke from the news at noon through
the local broadcast network's early p.m. programming block.
For hours I served as a silent juror on civil disputes of money
and debt, property, housing, injury, marriage, and custody. As
I got older and increasing daytime commitments pulled me
away from television screens, I'd find episodes online. Later, I
binged them on streaming services. These countless cases became an education. Today, I am an expert in avoiding certain
adult complications. I'll never cosign for anyone. I take metic-
ulous pictures whenever I move in or out of a rental. I don't
borrow money that's more than a quarter of my paycheck. I
don't loan anything I can't live without. I'm wary of those who
offer to pay me when their tax refund arrives.

I know how reality court shows work. I'm aware they
are spectacles constructed to gain advertisement revenue.

Producers scan circuit court records across the nation for the most interesting and volatile cases. The plaintiffs are offered a chance for financial compensation. These shows award the winner the monetary judgment determined by the verdict. The defendant is absolved of all responsibility to pay. The stakes then are low. Still, I'm enamored of these real-life court dramas. A thrill rolls down my spine when a litigant's flaws are somehow obscured to themselves. Pity rocks my chest when insufficient evidence allows a callous narcissist to walk away without consequence. I used to think my attraction to these shows was a matter of voyeurism, a reflection of my baseness. Eventually, I realized that whenever Judith Sheindlin reminds the court that, "If it doesn't make sense, it's usually not true," or when Faith Jenkins chastises someone while maintaining her beauty pageant poise, or when Joseph Blakeney Brown Jr. chuckles to himself over an absurd claim, I can believe in a system of justice. For thirty minutes, I'm presented with impartial and objective rulings. The race, creed, and nationality of the litigants never appears to influence the judicator's decision. The verdicts are not always fair, in the moral sense, but cruelty and ignorance are always rebuked by the judges. I return time and time again to these robed television personalities, like a child looking for a trusted adult to take my hand and tell me I'm going to be okay. Someone with answers in unlawful situations.

One might wish to believe the law is some neutral space outside of the prejudices and hierarchies that shape our daily lives. It isn't. The law is not divorced from the population that upholds it. A society founded on racism will adopt laws that reflect its founding. It is recursive. No matter how pragmatic a lawyer or a judge might seem, it isn't possible to divorce a proponent of the law from its practice. The referee does not have a job without the game. However, syndicated television arbitrations don't reflect many of the realities of the American legal system. These shows are a great comfort as life continually reveals to me that the law is not on my side. They are a fantasy too alluring not to indulge.

I think these shows provided a release for my maternal grandmother, too. Being born the daughter of a freed slave, and raised through Jim Crow and segregation, she had an intimate knowledge of the ways justice could fail her. My grandmother was known for calling out unjust bullshit whenever she encountered it. She was involved in many civil, and not so civil, disputes with family, friends, and strangers. I bet whenever she was cheated, beaten, cut, or shot at, whenever she felt unprotected by the law, she fantasized about an arbitrator whose impartiality was ensured by millions of viewers. I inherited that desire and appreciation for daytime television from her, in addition to her temper and a taste for boiled cabbage.

16

"Dem free-niggers f'um de N'of am sho' crazy."

17. UNDERTOW

Walking across campus at the Bangkok university where I teach, a familiar swell of pointlessness wraps around my neck and yanks me down onto my knees. In front of the university Communication Arts building, I choke and sputter, fumbling to loosen my tie and the invisible noose constricting my throat. When I manage to stand again, I thank a group of concerned New Media students who, although en route to other classes, stopped to offer assistance.

I paddle through the rest of the day.

I'm fine...

Until reading a friend's article on sea slavery in Southeast Asia prompts me to consider how my complacency plays a role in violations against the freedom of others.

And I debate throwing myself from a moving taxi on the Bang Na Expressway.

Nah...I'm good.

Until, while waiting on the Sky Train platform, I notice a poster advertisement for distilled water and I think about the number of disposable plastic bottles I've contributed to the tons of floating garbage congesting the planet's waterways.

And I visualize jumping onto the rails as the train arrives.

I can't stop thinking of the burden of my existence.

The guilt comes with desire to absolve myself. And because I can never do enough to make up for my part in the degradation of the world, never do enough to excuse the amount of chocolate I've consumed from global food conglomerates profiting from child labor, never do enough to pardon the amount of fossil fuels burned in frequent flyer miles, my own demise often seems the easiest way to excuse myself.

Usually, I can keep busy enough to ignore the tug of futility, drown myself in work and creative projects to prevent my mind from dwelling on my own ineffectiveness. I've developed habits to keep my thoughts shallow before they sink to darker depths. *Focus on what's next. Keep kicking to the next day, next hour, minute, second.* I go through the motions of being someone with a purpose. But a month after submitting my first personal essay collection to my publisher, I'm flooded with feelings of worthlessness.

My Thai spouse picks me up from the train station, and we talk on the ride home.

"Nothing is forever. So there isn't much point, right? Everything will be destroyed, eventually, even the Earth which I am helping to kill just by sticking around."

P, my partner, sighs. She doesn't take her eyes off the road to address me, "So what do you want to do?"

"Well, I've been thinking more seriously about killing myself."

The words tumble out of my mouth before I can stop them. I offer a soft chuckle, and P glances over to return my expectant stare.

She grins nervously and replies, "No."

"What do you mean?" I ask.

She repeats herself, still smiling, "Fuck you, no. You can't kill yourself."

"I can't stop fretting over how print copies of the essay collection might contribute, however little, to deforestation."

"What?"

"Does writing a book about my own experience only benefit myself?"

I continue trying to articulate my doubt. Once I've

exhausted myself, P admits she doesn't know how to help me. She asks if I've considered talking to a professional.

"No."

"Why?"

I pause, catch myself before I reply: *Because my people don't do therapy.*

I can recognize the fallacy of this statement and how it would come across as an oversimplification. I mean to articulate to P that my family raised me to think of psychoanalysis as a last resort. Psychiatrists serve folks who can't get right. People like my uncle Cloudy.

When I was a kid, my grandmother warned me not to make loud noises around Uncle Cloudy. She said I shouldn't move too quickly or walk too close behind him. She said Uncle Cloudy had come in contact with Agent Orange while fighting in a jungle in Vietnam, and he came out of the service all messed up. As I got older, I'd learn that Uncle Cloudy's exposure to toxic herbicides didn't fully explain his melancholy. When prayers for Uncle Cloudy didn't appear to curb his dark thoughts, the night terrors, or his talk about taking his own life, he started visiting a counselor at the Department of Veterans Affairs every so often.

Although I can hardly remember Uncle Cloudy's voice, I can recall being eight years old, sandwiched between Cloudy and my granduncle on the bench seat of an El Camino speeding down a country road. I no longer recollect our destination or where we had departed, but I still see Cloudy letting his arm roll up and down with the wind rushing past the open passenger-side window—fingers tight together, up like the flap of a plane wing, catching the breeze against his palm and raising his flat hand higher, then fingers curling downward on a wave of air. I remember seeing a familiar weariness in Uncle Cloudy's somber expression as he stared out into the blurring thickets of green kudzu. I liked spending time in Uncle Cloudy's company, being still together, perhaps sensing a shared sadness.

When someone discovered Uncle Cloudy's body stretched across a walkway beneath an Atlanta overpass, it made sense to me. Family members suspected a nefarious force behind his purported suicide. They said he made good money from his monthly disability checks, and someone might have robbed him and then pushed him to his death. *Because we just don't kill ourselves*, I heard some whisper after the burial. *We persevered through segregation and slavery and the Middle Passage. We endure, with God's help.*

Whenever I felt despondent growing up, my parents and elders would tell me to take my struggles to the Lord in prayer. Pastors and clergy make themselves more readily available than therapists do. Plus, a tithe is cheaper than mental healthcare. When my mother gave birth to me in 1984, African Americans made up 11.7 percent of the population and their families accounted for 3 percent of the United States' $6 billion household wealth holdings. A decade later, African Americans represented a little over 12 percent of the population. While national household wealth had risen to over $9 billion, homes like mine were locked in at 3 percent. In 2019, the Federal Reserve found that white families, on average, had eight times the wealth of African American families. These numbers suggest that despite liberal ideals of how well society is advancing, many things aren't improving. Of course members of my family would find it difficult to justify spending hundreds of dollars to talk to a stranger when bills are due and a minister could listen for free.

"Maybe you're depressed," P says.

I repeat the word as a question, "Depressed?"

Who am I to have depression?

Around the globe, people who look like me suffer, thousands

die on journeys across seas and deserts to escape poverty, war, political persecution, and ecological disaster. Thousands die in pursuit of a fraction of what I possess. My mother always tells me, "Baby, you are blessed." Mom's sentiment feels true, riding in my spouse's hybrid car, thinking about the air emissions and environmental impact of the copper mining required to wire and power parts of the vehicle. *I stay blessed.* As we slow to a stop in gridlock traffic, I stare at my smartphone to avoid P's anxious gaze, and I scroll through news stories on suicide rates in an East Asian factory that builds components for the device in my hand. I wonder why everyone else can't be blessed, too.

I'm fine.

I'm good, comparatively, and healthy enough.

But am I well?

Do I deserve to be well?

My folks didn't talk about mental wellness. I suppose they were naturally skeptical of a social science once used to negate their humanity. Until the middle of the 1800s, people like me were believed to have immunity to mental illness. Mental health ideology and public policy largely dismissed the idea of my people developing mental disorders because we were viewed as property, like a tool, and tools don't get disheartened. This opinion changed with the Civil War and Southern Reconstruction in the USA. Many clinical professionals thought newly won freedom could harm the mental wellbeing of slaves. The conversation continued to pivot throughout the start of the twentieth century, and by the 1960s many believed Africans and communities of the diaspora—alleged to be morally and intellectually inferior to European races—were more susceptible to mental illness.

Later studies in the 1980s and '90s proved risk for developing a mental disorder had nothing to do with skin color or ethnicity, not on a physiological level. While people who look like me exceed all other American populations in admissions to psychiatric hospitals, this statistic has more to do with how one's skin color relates to common disparities in lived experience that can lead to depression, has more do with how pigmentation can relate to perpetual traumatic stress, and how societal expectations for people of color to endure suffering can inundate an individual with feelings of worthlessness.

The car moves again, and I ask myself, *Did I earn this guilt, or did I learn it?*

"Maybe I've been taught to feel sad all the time."

P replies, "Taught by who?"

"No one in particular."

Despite all the rationale shaping my bias, when P asks again why I won't go to a therapist, I have no answer for her.

We arrive home.

P parks under the carport.

We sit, silent, listening to the cooling engine emit soft clicks and wheezes.

She asks me, "Have you ever tried to kill yourself?"

And I don't enumerate the times I've pulled plastic bags over my head as a child, the times I'd try to smother/drown/choke/cut myself, or the destructive behavior throughout my adolescence and adulthood. I can't begin to tell P about the previous evening when I walked out onto a campus balcony and leaned over its cement wall eleven floors up until, much like all the earlier instances, a voice sounded in my head, *We Don't Kill Ourselves*, and my hands caught the ledge and I pulled myself back, my hands dropped the knife, my hands pulled the belt from my neck, yanked the pillow from my face.

"You know, if you killed yourself, you'd hurt me?" P says.

"I know."

Guilt pulls me down and lifts me up. I don't know who I am without it. Maybe I fear if I take steps to resolve my guilt and become content, I would lose the only version of myself I've ever known. Who am I without the guilt I've inherited?

P reminds me my death is of no use to anyone.

"I know," I say before exiting the car.

I'm not ready to swim out from beneath the swells, but I can assign myself purpose, and maybe by persisting I could unearth a means to give more than I take. Maybe I could author my own salvation.

Later, in bed but not asleep, I type in a frenzy as P snoozes next to me. I keep writing through the night on the manuscript soon due to my publisher. I don't stop until beams of sunlight stray through the space between the heavy window curtains. I don't allow myself rest. The work is a distraction from death. Maybe writing will allow me to unlearn my guilt. I hope to craft something useful, but it's no longer clear if it's for others or for myself.

But I keep going, to the next second...next minute...hour... day, then maybe another.

18.

Every day, fear being made into a hashtag. Every day...

19.

I have heard them label my uncle a bootlegger,

sold booze without the mob to ease the pain of others.

20

"I pictured in my mind a white God listening to me praying. And I wondered if he cared anything about a little colored boy's prayers..."

21.

I hear the women say, "These niggas are trifling."

"They are all dogs," they say. "A nigga can't be trusted."

I'm up next at the barbershop. I pause Jay-Z's "4:44," remove my headphones, and seat myself in Joe's chair.

"How goes it, professor? How you want it done today?"

"Cut it close all around but keep it dark. Thank you."

Joe gets to cutting. One of the other barbers is complaining about the influx of young Caucasian men coming to get their hair trimmed and faded.

"It's like got-damn dog hair," he exclaims. "It gets everywhere and you can't brush or wash it off. Not like our hair. Ours goes down the drain."

He mimes scrubbing furiously after a shower. All the customers and other barbers chuckle, nodding. I try hard not to giggle with Joe's clippers shearing my head.

In the lull that follows the laughter, Joe asks me how I've been.

I tell him I'm getting a divorce.

He sucks his teeth and shakes his head. He says it happens and he's sorry to hear it. "She seemed nice," Joe says.

Someone referencing P in the past tense shakes me. I shift

uncomfortably underneath the smock buttoned around my neck. I don't want to think of her as something to cut and discard, like the severed strands raining from my scalp onto the checkered floor.

I ask Joe how long he's been married.

"Thirty-eight years," he replies over the buzz of the clippers. "I love that woman."

"You ever cheat on her?"

Joe replies confidently, "No."

I wonder what's wrong with me.

Another barber picks up on my conversation with Joe and asks, "Thirty-eight years and you never cheated?"

Again, Joe says no. "Been with her since I was twenty-one."

P and I met when we were both twenty-one.

Joe says, "Why would I go and do something stupid to mess that up?"

The room begins to snicker.

A customer getting the edges of his beard shaped addresses Joe.

"Now, it's good to try and be faithful and all that, but there's got to have been some temptation after thirty years of being with the same woman."

Another chimes in. "Me and my girl are doing good. I haven't cheated since the start of the new year."

We all laugh. It's the first week of February.

The bearded brother continues, "Abraham had many wives. A man is a man. God put more women than men on the Earth for a reason. It's bound to happen. You know what I'm saying?"

I don't know, not fully.

Folks go on chatting about the differences God established between men and women, Joe lines the top of my forehead, and I consider the dissonance between my thoughts and actions, how I could betray the trust of a woman I love, while also wanting so desperately to be as committed as Joe.

x

P and I married when we were 25. When I asked P to marry me, I vowed to make it work no matter what. I'd be faithful. I would not cheat, like I had in all of my earlier relationships. We'd be an interracial power couple to which others would aspire.

Together we started a Thai food restaurant, bought a car and a house, expatriated from the United States to Thailand, helped her family launch an international auto parts supply company, and even considered adoption. P was a great partner, and I had every intention of spending my life with her, of committing to my marriage, even when it was clear we growing apart and building separate lives. I ignored the fact that in our last years together we rarely touched each other. I didn't interrogate why we both remained so insistent on keeping separate bank accounts, or how neither of us expressed frustration with living in separate spaces most weeks (me in an apartment provided by my university just outside of Bangkok, and her on the other end of the city at her father's house). I didn't stop to question what it signaled when I applied for a professorship in Nagoya, Japan, without telling P first, or what it meant when she didn't protest the possibility of me leaving.

I would have never acknowledged how aspects of my marriage made me feel lonely if, on January 1st, 2017, I hadn't received a Facebook message from one of my mother's cousins letting me know my mother had been hospitalized. I returned to America, unsure what to expect. I found my mother in terrible condition, but slowly coming back to life. Her home was condemned. She would never be able to live alone again. I am her only son, and I became her caregiver. The distance between P and me was greater and more indefinite than ever. In this separation, gaps between the spouse I wished to be and what I really yearned for became unavoidable.

In most of my earlier relationships I struggled to stay committed to one person. I had difficulty not wanting to be wanted. It didn't matter if I was already in a monogamous relationship. I feared losing the attention, the feeling of being beautiful and coveted. By the time I met and married P, I had begun to understand that my tendency to cheat on people I cared for was a reflection of my self-esteem. When you feel like an undesirable person, perhaps you are more inclined to risk the promise of fidelity for immediate affection. My negative feelings about myself could hurt others. I vowed never to fail P the same way.

So there was a terrible sense of guilt and disappointment when, during the eight months away from my partner, I started craving affection from someone new. At first, I rationalized: flirting with a friend online is not the same as adultery. I wasn't sleeping with anyone. But soon, as the conversations grew deeper and more personal, I began to suspect myself of emotional infidelity. I felt like I was letting P down every day I fantasized about being with another person. Asking P for a divorce remains the hardest thing I have ever done, but I was certain she deserved more than I could give her.

Not long after asking to end our marriage, I pursued a connection with another person and we started dating. P felt blindsided, angry, deceived, and disillusioned. She knew my passwords for everything and searched through my email and social media for proof of infidelity. P sent screenshots of intimate messages between me and the person I was dating to some of my friends and family.

Many of the women in my life confirmed that I had lied by omission. Seeing another woman before P and I could legally end our marriage was a deception.

"You couldn't wait until the divorce was final?" asked my mother, my stepmother, my female friends, and my half-sisters.

"You've engaged in some fuckboy behavior," one of my sisters said.

"I don't approve of that shit," said the other sister.

The pair of them read me. They told me about myself. When they finished, they each reminded me they loved me, but they were disappointed.

That disappointment—being viewed in an instant like dudes who had failed my sisters' love—nearly killed me. To others, I had become a caricature: the bad boyfriend in Erykah Badu's "Tyrone," the disappointing rollin' stone dad The Temptations sang about, every other man who has led a woman to shout in exasperation, "niggas are trifling."

I asked my sisters, "How ubiquitous is the expression, 'trifling-ass nigga,' and what does it mean to each of you?"

My oldest sister laughed. "It is very common. I can't describe it without repeating the same phrase. It's kind of like a dusty bitch."

My youngest sister said, "I don't know why or how, but that describes it perfectly! It's the dude who slides into your DMs and his profile picture is of him and his girlfriend."

"A fuckboy?" I said.

"Bingo!" said the eldest sister.

The youngest sister continued, "A fuckboy, to me, is a low-budget player. He leads you on, and presumably a bunch of other women, for sport or because he's particularly suave. However, he's too immature to be honest with you or himself. He doesn't know how to responsibly deal with his own loneliness, so he uses women to temporarily fill his empty spaces. And he has just enough access to a good barber and the internet to look and sound like a guy you'd want to be with."

Recognizing some of my own behavior in her description, the possibility that I might be seen as someone I had tried so desperately not to be, punched air from my lungs.

x

Why couldn't I make my marriage with P work? Why couldn't I resist my attraction to another person? And why wasn't the fear of letting down ideals I had about a religious sacrament enough to stop me? Does being African American make me more prone to ruin romantic partnerships? Why is cheating so commonly associated with Black men?

I'm not sure there are definitive answers to these questions. Infidelity isn't exclusive to one particular race. I know this. However, popular American music, movies, TV, and literature promote infidelity as pathological in men of a certain race.

P and I loved watching daytime tabloid talk shows together. We'd spend weekends in bed, bingeing full episodes of *The Maury Show* posted on YouTube. I often feared the prevalence of

African American guests on the program might lead P to believe men of my race were predisposed to cheating.

The segments are familiar:

I had a recording, Maury...you could hear sex noises and oohs and aahs...I found these panties in my bedroom...I found these panties under a seat in his car, Maury...I can't fit these...I can't wear these little-ass draws, Maury...I found numerous pictures in his phone... inappropriate messages from females on Facebook...mysterious stains on his clothes...on his car seats...on our bed...he comes home smelling like sex...our sex is different, Maury...I know he's lying to me...after these results, he's gone...after these results, I'm through... after these results...he's going to have to get up out of my house.

The studio audience welcomes the accused men to the stage with a chorus of boos and jeers. The male guests wave away the disapproval of the angry crowd before giving an explanation.

She's crazy...she's emotional...look, don't get me wrong, in the beginning of the relationship I messed up a lot, but that was the past and she won't let it go...I'm a good man...I love this woman...I get home from hustling every day and she's sniffing all over me...she's going all through my pockets...she's searching all through my car...through my phone...I'm a good man...

Eventually, the host, Maury Povich, reaches for a large tan envelope, handed to him by a cameraperson or a production assistant waiting in the gap between the spectators and the stage.

I have the test results right here, Maury says. *You were asked, other than what she knows about, during your relationship, have you ever had sexual contact of any kind with any other woman. You answered no. The lie detector test determined...that was a lie...you were asked, do you purposefully ignore her calls because you're out with another woman. You said no. The lie detector test determined that was a lie...You were asked, during your relationship, if you ever had sexual intercourse with any other women who text message your phone...you admitted to our lie detector administrator that you did.*

The men dispute the results while the women they've betrayed scream in frustration and disappointment.

Really?...Really?...Go be with those dusty-ass bitches, then. You're a dog.

Ralph Barbieri, the lie detector administrator, appears beside the stage to confirm the test results and divulge observations of deception during the polygraph.

Moments later, backstage, Executive Producer Paul Faulhaber tries to get the male guests to fully admit their transgressions. Paul intercedes on behalf of the adulterous men. He appeals to the female guests, encouraging forgiveness and marital duty not unlike Paul of Tarsus in letters to the Corinthians. Often Maury comes behind the sound stage to aid Paul, especially if the couple shares children. Many times, the duo succeeds in convincing the guests to stay together.

P would shake her head disapprovingly.

"The dude's just going to do it again," she'd say.

And I'd nod in agreement, the both of us choosing to forget or ignore how much my behavior in previous relationships mirrored those guys on *Maury* who were incapable of faithfulness.

x

Statistical information does not often help to dispel the image of African American males fearful of long-term commitment. Concluding years of quantitative research into African American marriages in the twentieth century, Elaine B. Pinderhughes, professor emerita at the Boston College School of Social Work, claimed African American males "exhibit infidelity at a rate higher than other groups, and are nearly twice as likely to be unfaithful as white men." Supporting this assertion, results from a national behavioral survey conducted by the *American Journal of Public Health* revealed a higher rate of infidelity among African Americans than white Americans.

But I ponder the causes of this data. The numbers reflected in these studies couldn't possibly encompass the intersections and nuances that shape the population being observed, factors both universal and singular. These stats fail to examine what precedes them or identify what shapes their evidence.

I don't claim to be able to provide this insight. I've got no easy answers. Anything I come up with beyond my own experience would just be speculation. I'm not sure there is a way to explain the countless reasons why anyone does anything. We contain multitudes. Human behavior is infinitely complex.

I'm still learning to explain why I've cheated in the past and why I was tempted to betray my marriage before I could legally end it. I think it probably involves a weird mix of patriarchal religious beliefs common among my community and my overexposure to mass media narratives that stigmatized fatness while reinforcing white beauty standards.

Growing up, I often heard "You'd be handsome..."

If I didn't eat so much.

If I didn't let my skin get too dark.

Growing up, in the shows and movies I'd watch, kids my size were comic relief. Boys my color were funny best friends of the white protagonist. They were not lovers. I'd listen to the Notorious B.I.G. call himself a true player, but never felt comfortable imagining myself throwing my hands in the air in solidarity. Mainstream narratives did nothing to convince me I might be someone to desire. Inundated with globally distributed media of men like me failing to embrace the love they think they deserve, I'm not sure I could have ever fully learned to receive or give devotion.

x

Months leading up to my divorce, I thought a lot about the religious stories I had been taught when I was a young boy. In the Bible, Abraham did have many wives. Lamech took two wives, Adah and Zillah. Ashur, the father of Tekoa, had two wives, Helah and Naarah. Jehoiada had two wives as well. At forty, Esau married Judith and Basemath, and later Mahalath. King Solomon loved many foreign women, Moabite, Ammonite, Edomite, Sidonian, Hittite women, and even the daughter of a pharaoh. Rehoboam had eighteen wives and sixty concubines, fathering twenty-eight sons and sixty daughters. David took more and more wives at Jerusalem, and he became the father of more sons and daughters. I wondered if I'd be forgiven by the god of these men, or condemned by failing to honor matrimony. Admittedly, I've always struggled with God's unconditional love, the idea I might have been born into grace.

Believing I should ever be loved despite my humanity became even harder, rereading mournful text messages from P in quiet hours of existential dread.

[12 November]

The man I thought would never hurt me

The man I thought was different than other men

The man I always looked up to

No longer exists or he was just really good at pretending

I dwell on the final lines of P's goodbye...

All your friends think you are a good person

but look at what you've done

If you can hurt me this deeply

If you can cheat on me

There are no good people.

x

I'm angry with myself, but also with societal expectations that turn my faults and failings into affirmations of racial stereotypes. With P, I had wanted so desperately to break out of a monolith, to avoid further contributing to a typecast of Black noncommitment.

The last time I saw P as my wife was in Los Angeles. She flew in from Thailand, and I had arrived from South Carolina. I was going to give a reading at a bookstore, and we met before the event to make a divorce plan. We signed papers and traded items we wanted the other to keep. That night I read a piece about wandering Bangkok and how she made that city a home for me. The moment I got off stage I looked for her. I found her weeping alone among the stacks. I pulled her into a hug and we cried together. I apologized for everything, for hiding so much of myself from her, for falling in love with someone else before our legal separation, for allowing my fear of reinforcing stereotypes to prevent me from sharing my feelings of isolation with her, for keeping us in a marriage that didn't give her everything she needed.

x

Seated on a log of sunbaked driftwood, resting on a shore of pebbles, I stare over the Pacific Ocean and think of the home I left on the other side of the sea.

I think of a text P sent me earlier in the day. She wrote to me about finding a connection with someone new. She had anxiety heading into their second meeting.

And I responded:

[20 February]

You'll be fine.

Remember,

He's lucky to be on a date with you.

Looking at the white caps crashing over the northwestern waves, I pray silently. I say thanks to my divine maker for the beauty in front of me. I say thanks for the respite offered by the fallen, tide-stripped tree; thanks for the erosion that formed the dozen sea stacks on the water's horizon, and all the quakes and eruptions that bred the millions of tiny rocks below my feet.

I give reverence for all the stunning things that came from cracks and faults.

I pray for forgiveness from whatever higher power, and from myself, that I might one day recognize a similar majesty in my own brokenness.

And I pray P's date goes well, that she finds someone who loves her the way I know she deserves, the way I could not.

I feel a hand press against my shoulder.

I turn to the woman sitting beside me.

I study this woman's face, rosy from the sea winds charging toward the Cascade Range. I think to myself, *I want to be someone who makes her happy*. I never want to betray the way she looks back at me, how she seems to peer into my past, present, and future all at once. I want to honor this woman's gaze.

I'm moving past the guilt and disappointment of my first marriage; forward, not over it. I'm not interested in being committed to a person just because I'm trying to prove an idea wrong. I want to live more honestly, learning how to deal more responsibly with my own loneliness, knowing I am someone who deserves to give and receive devotion.

We sit silently, watching her young son dance over clumps

of sea foam scattered along the stony beach.

Her fingers slide down my arm and intertwine with mine.

I squeeze back.

The boy ventures closer to the water, throwing rocks and giggling at the splash.

23.

Every day?

[24.]

"This is the afterlife of slavery—skewed life chances, limited access to health and education, premature death, incarceration, and impoverishment. I, too, am the afterlife of slavery."

Listen. When the flashing lights appear behind us, I'll move slowly to retrieve my ID from my wallet. Keep your hands gripped firmly on the wheel. Don't make any sudden movements as the man in uniform approaches. I will ask if you have a phone number for my relatives in case you need to notify them of my arrest, or in case of worse.

When the police officer arrives at your driver-side door, you will want to argue. Don't. As he leans down to speak across your chest, requesting my license before accepting yours, resist the urge to question him. Once he retreats to his cruiser to cross-check my name against criminal databases, you'll speculate reasons the officer chose to signal us.

Maybe your sedan fits the description of a vehicle police are looking for.

Maybe I fit the description of a suspect.

He will have offered no immediate explanation, so we can only guess.

A persistent doubting will always skew aspects of our interactions in public.

I'll scan past the windows for anyone outside who might serve as witness. I'll mention any security or traffic cameras pointed in the vicinity of the car. *You'll need to remember them.* I won't have to explain why.

When the officer returns to us, he'll ask you to step out of the car. You'll ask to know why, and he'll inform you that your front vehicle registration plate is displayed incorrectly. He'll point to the flat metal tag propped between your dashboard and windshield instead of mounted to the sloping nose of your car. He'll cite state law. And with your pale skin flushed red, you'll ask if he's serious. You've driven with your license plate in your front window for over a year. He'll assure you of his sincerity, reaching for his handcuffs. He'll even apologize. He'll hope you understand. He has a job to do.

You'll remind him of the dates and address on your driver's license: *today is your birthday / you're only half a mile from home / friends and family are expecting you.*

You'll remind the officer of your young son, watching, frozen, in the backseat.

But the officer has a job, and he hopes you, and your son, will understand.

The officer won't be totally unsympathetic. He'll cuff your hands in front of your body before walking you over to his county sheriff vehicle. He'll guide you into the front passenger side, not the caged backseat.

When the officer has you in custody, he'll instruct me to get out of your car. With a hand hovering near the weapon on his belt, he'll wait for me to exit and walk around to the driver side. I'll be close enough then to read the name on the badge pinned to his chest.

He'll return my license and I'll thank him.

I'll hate myself for thanking him.

I'll use his name after every directive he gives because I heard somewhere using their name humanizes me to law enforcement, because I heard somewhere using their title and name reinforces that I acknowledge and acquiesce to the officer's authority, because I heard repeating their name lets them know I'm paying attention.

Because I've been told countless techniques for how to survive encounters with police.

The officer will tell me to drive the car. He'll leave me responsible for your son during the short drive to your house. And as the officer departs, he'll encourage me to *be careful*.

After he leaves with you, I'll start the car.

Your son will finally exhale. He'll stare down at his empty hands trying to solve an invisible puzzle. I'll take rural roads to your house, debating what to do next. I'll swallow rising waves of guilt, damming the urge to scream apologies at your son.

I'm not sure I will ever know how to fully articulate my contrition for the way things are. I don't know where to begin to say I'm sorry for the way in which my body is viewed by others, or how those perceptions put you in jeopardy.

x

I memorize the details following your arrest, in case I'm asked.

I drove to your mother's house and left your son with her. I promised them both I'd bring you home. I Googled the address of the county jail and mapped the quickest way there while avoiding major thoroughfares. On the way to you, I counted every other car I saw without a license plate above its front bumper: dozens. I parked a block from the downtown detention center. I practiced smiles and nods of affirmation in the rearview mirror.

I had never entered a correctional facility by choice. It felt alien pulling open the heavy doors of metal and bulletproof polymer. I walked past rows of morose civilians staring vacantly at the floor or ceiling, or glaring at a single wall clock posted above the reception window.

I approached the intercom and waited to be noticed. Several seconds passed before the two officers on the other side of the glass paused their conversation to press the button that would allow us to communicate through the clear barrier. The officer wore a Kevlar vest over his sleeveless shirt. He grunted a stern and expecting "Yeah?"

I explained why I had come, and he was helpful.

He pointed past the glass, to a machine resembling an ATM in the corner of the waiting area. The device performed several functions, including the ability to credit funds to jailed family, friends, or lovers. He told me that once you were processed into the system after booking, the facility would assign you a number, and I could use that identification number to add money to your commissary, improve your accommodations, or pay bail money to secure your release.

The bare-armed officer checked for your name against a list of arrests. I studied the cop's tattoos as he worked. His skin bore Chinese characters, an assortment of flames, and a grey-scale American flag with a single streak of blue. Slathered in healing ointment, the dark nationalism stretching the length and the width of his upper right arm shined under the harsh fluorescent lighting.

I am familiar with that variation of the flag as a symbol for Blue Lives Matter, a countermovement to groups campaigning for the end of systemic racism and violence. A Blue Lives Matter flag signifies to me that in response to my pleas for equality, in response to my demand for peace, when I say, "I am dying every day unlawfully," there are those eager to reply, "Well, I could die, too." As if there is any comparison between the disproportionate death and incarceration experienced by African Americans born into a racist society, and those who have suffered in their chosen occupation. The Blue Lives Matter flag provides the same warning to me as a Confederate Flag: If they are present, I should not be. And whatever plight I might experience due to my skin color is no match for the flagbearer's pride.

And so the ink on the officer's arm colors our entire interaction. I can only debate the inferences of his politeness when he informed me that you had already arrived at the receiving area and that you would be preceded by a long line of others apprehended before you. The officer told me it would be hours before I could get you out of jail.

I thanked the officer before turning away to find an empty seat among the waiting, forlorn faces.

x

Being held against one's will prompts contemplation. There is little else to do.

Even from the outside, the hours following your apprehension provided time to contemplate the automation of incarceration; like the 13th Amendment of the US Constitution, where the promise of freedom from slavery is offered, then denied with the loophole of incarceration. All the brilliant ways that have been divined to legally turn a person into a commodity.

When your name finally appeared in the system on the jail ATM, I inserted my credit card and withdrew it quickly as instructed. I paid the bail and agreed to the additional convenience fees. The machine printed a receipt and asked for my email to send a digital proof of purchase for your release. I took the slip of paper to the reception desk. The officer I had spoken to earlier had been replaced by someone new. I slid the receipt through a thin slit beneath the bulletproof glass. He examined the small paper and explained that the jail was in the process of a shift change. It would take a little while before all the incoming guards arrived to relieve those currently inside the precinct.

I told him I understood, and he returned the receipt to me.

As I turned from the window I was compelled through the lobby of the jail, through the revolving doors, and out onto the large steps of the detention center. Once outside I became aware of my breathing, the warm, soft wind rushing over my lips, the oxygen pulling into my lungs and through my extremities and up to my brain.

I thought of you and imagined what you might be experiencing. I thought about the last time I was arrested. In the back seat of the cop car, I wiggled and shifted to take the pressure off my hands cuffed behind my back. My weight threated to dislocate my arms every time the vehicle hit a bump. Eventually I learned to lean forward to relieve the pressure. My face hovered inches from the thick polymer window that separated me from the officer, for their safety. At the county jail, the officer guided me out of the cruiser and into a booking area. I was photographed, finger printed, and then led into a large cell. The cinder-block wall opposite the metal door jutted out to form a long bench. The ground sloped to a wide circular drain at its center. Rows of long fluorescent bulbs covered the ceiling of the concrete room, casting a blueish haze over the grey space. A single stainless-steel toilet stood in the corner. I considered joining the men scattered along the bench, but I opted instead to sit with my legs folded on the ground by the entrance. There were no clocks or windows in the cell. There was no way to determine the passing of time but the arrival of food: bologna on plain white bread with a cup of water, slid into the room on thin aluminum trays, a sandwich and drink for each prisoner. Some of the men chattered as they ate, sharing their various charges and offenses. I stayed quiet but one man seemed very curious about my presence there. I announced my charge, "a breach of the peace," and they all nodded, content with no further details. The men spoke a little more, speculating on what verdicts they might face from the judge in the morning. Eventually they returned to silence. In the absence of their voices, I noticed the steady rumble of the A/C unit and how, despite the cold, stale air being pumped into the space, I felt suffocated. Thinking about my own impending sentence, about the cost of my bail, freedom vs. prison, and how I might navigate being detained indefinitely, I felt my body forgetting to breathe.

Outside of the jail that held you, I watched dusk begin to peel back the day. I breathed deeply, tasting minute shifts in the air. I saw hints of the moon making its ascent, and I thought of you in a cell like the one I remember: a confined space absent of time and breeze and light. I thought about my guilt and gratitude to stand outside of the jail instead of locked inside it. I contemplated the ways your detention complicated my freedom.

x

Once dusk faded to night, I returned to the lobby. I continued waiting for you: an ebbing tension churning my stomach, crashing heavy on my shoulders, and throbbing vessels around my temples. I chose an empty seat facing the jail ATM and tried not to focus on all the money being fed into the machine. But I was drawn to the backs of people shaking their heads, fumbling through their purses and pockets. The flow of bodies began to bleed together, until someone said, "Hey, you know how to work this thing?"

After several seconds I realized the woman standing at the jail ATM was asking me for assistance. I nodded.

She didn't wait for me to inquire about her situation before launching into her complaint: "I'm trying to put money on my man's phone card or whatever, and this stupid thing doesn't tell me if it went through or not."

I rose to my feet and moved to her.

She stepped aside, released a puff of frustration, and then sucked her teeth.

As I studied the jail ATM, poking at the screen, the woman shifted her attention to a small boy who was inching farther away from her and closer to the precinct's reception window. The boy's chin and nose resembled the woman's. I presumed she was his mother when she called out for him to return to her side and stay away from trouble.

"Like his daddy. Always getting into something," she said to me, or to herself, or to anyone.

"I think I figured it out," I said. "Your payment went through. It wants to know if you want your receipt printed or emailed to you." The authority in my voice surprised me. Only a few hours earlier I was like the mother, confused and frustrated. Waiting had made me a veteran. My disorientation was replaced by alternating weariness and frenzy.

"I want it emailed," she replied.

I took a step away from the jail ATM, and she started typing her email address. We traded our focus. I watched her son while she worked with the machine—by virtue of being on this side of the plexiglass we'd become partners. The little boy made no progress toward his mother. He swayed gently, his legs and feet still not fully adept at carrying his frame. I thought the boy looked no older than four. He had the same skin color as me. I followed the line of his gaze to a pair of officers chatting behind the thick glass enclosing the reception desk. The boy stared at them intently.

My toes curled in my shoes. My lower back felt damp. I cleared my throat, preparing to call the boy back to his mother, but I wasn't sure how to address him and feared consequences for shouting. Before I could speak, a young, white officer entered the lobby from a door bordering the reception window. The top button of this uniform was unclasped, and he carried a YMCA duffle bag loosely over his shoulder. He smiled, moving steadily to exit the building. He was on a path that would collide with the boy.

I was held in place by an invisible hand.

The officer noticed the boy watching the reception desk. He

stopped to loom over the child, and the child looked up to meet the officer's eyes.

I panicked for the boy, but the child studied the cop, unaware of any danger. The officer said hello, and the boy watched him rustle through the duffle bag and remove a sticker. The young officer knelt to let the boy examine an adhesive sheriff's badge before peeling it from its paper and pressing it to the boy's chest.

As a kid, I often wanted to grow up to join law enforcement. I wanted to protect and serve like Carl Winslow, the patient patriarch on the television show *Family Matters*. I wanted to defeat those who would threaten the lives of the innocent, to be a hero despite my flaws, like detectives Marcus Burnett and Mike Lowrey in *Bad Boys* or Axel Foley in *Beverly Hills Cop*. I might have become a police officer if the world beyond these films didn't teach me how real officers must also enforce laws that disenfranchise entire populations. But if I had become a policeman, I'd hope to be like the young, white officer in front of me at that moment, extending a palm to the little boy to slap hands in a high-five.

The officer rose to his feet. He told the boy to take care. He resumed his march to exit the building, smiling at me and the boy's mother, telling both of us to have a good night as he passed.

As soon as he disappeared through the revolving doors of the precinct lobby, the mother rushed to her son. She collected her boy in her arms. The child ran his fingers over the pointed gold star stuck to the front of his T-shirt. His mother chided him for wandering too far from her and carried him out of the police station.

x

When you finally emerge from the receiving area, I'll reach a hand out to you, hoping to pull you into a hug, but you'll steam past me, furious. You'll lead us outside walking fast before you stop to ask me where I parked.

We won't speak again until we reach the car. You'll ask that I drive because you're shaking with rage. With you safe in the passenger seat, I'll crank the engine and it will rumble to life. That's when I'll notice you crying.

Through gritted teeth you'll say, "I'm sorry."

You'll repeat it again, over and over.

I'll apologize, too, wiping tears from your cheeks with my thumbs.

We'll forget for a moment that we have nothing to apologize for.

You will ask me to take rural roads back to your house. On the drive we'll fall silent again, perhaps both thinking about the motivations behind your arrest earlier that day. Perhaps both of us will wonder if I held your birthday bouquet a little too high in the passenger seat that morning, if the flowers I bought you were a little too bright. Maybe you'll wonder if you were grinning a little too wide before the officer stopped us, if you beamed a little too broadly.

You can hypothesize forever, fret yourself sick speculating about what we could have done to diminish our appearance together, to make ourselves less visible in the flashing of lights.

You'll think differently about what it means to see and be seen.

You'll become more vigilant.

You'll ponder new ways to dampen what wants so desperately to glow.

26. SKIT

FADE IN:

EXT. CORNER OF TIGER AVE & CONLEY AVE - DAY

Donald is walking toward the library to work on this manuscript. He is listening to music when he notices the end of a routine traffic stop. The officer is a white male. The driver of an egg-colored sport utility vehicle is dark-skinned. Donald slows down. He removes one of his headphones and watches the scene.

                    POLICE OFFICER

                     Here you go.

The police officer passes a moving violation ticket to the driver and then returns to his cruiser.

The driver sees Donald and rolls down the passenger-side window.

A beat.

> THE DRIVER
> (to Donald)
> Hey bruh!

> DONALD
> Hey...You okay?

A beat.

> THE DRIVER
> (chuckles nervously)
> I'm triggered.

A beat.

                         DONALD

                  (laughs nervously)

                  Yeah. Me, too.

     FADE OUT.

27.

I hear them shouting every day not to be made ghosts.

    These spirits sound like me, echoes only asking for better.

[28.]

"The limits of your ambition were, thus, expected to be set forever. You were born into a society which spelled out with brutal clarity, and in as many ways as possible, that you were a worthless human being. You were not expected to aspire to excellence: you were expected to make peace with mediocrity."

29.

Every day! Is it possible to live a free life of free will while bound between the borders of an American myth?

[30.]

"Yes, I did see him to have a weapon...It was his body."

31

Every day, bend and bow.

32.

Heard them report my cousin as a substance addict,

    on beat between crack dens, from one stint to another.

[33.]

"Please, cut the fucking shit, okay. Okay? When I go to the money machine tonight, I ain't looking over my back for the media; I'm looking for niggas. Shit Ted Koppel ain't never took shit from me. Niggas have. You think I have three guns in my house because the media's outside?"

Been thinking a little bit.

Remembering the homeboy at the literary conference.

Ripped, dread-head, heart-pump-diesel looking brother, call himself a poet.

Posturing, all sorry-not-sorry, in a red tee two sizes too small.

The shirt with the bold Helvetica quote from seven-year-old Latarian Milton.

Read, "I just wanna do hoodrat stuff with my friends" across the chest.

Probably not really fretting over dude, but his shirt.

What the shirt means. The intention.

Don't know. Bugging a little bit.

Remembering lil cuz, Robbie.

Robbie didn't relate to me genealogically.

Play cousins.

Our families were close.

Cuz grew up in the 'burbs around the way from my mother's

townhouse in Montgomery County, Maryland.

But I met Robbie one summer when we both happened to be visiting our grandmothers in a small town in South Carolina. Robbie taught me to twist my fingers into gang signs, bend my digits to spell out B-L-O-O-D.

Taught me how to strip a Swisher, pack and roll a blunt.

Robbie guided me through the darkest parts of the Southside on bicycles, stopping to chat with older boys gathered on corners.

Some lil pups are thirsty for juice.

Most days those corner boys told Robbie and me to leave, but sometimes they sent us both to fetch snacks from a gas station or convenience store. Whenever they got bored, they invited Robbie and me to join them. They instructed us on how to walk and talk, how to stand to fight. They taught me softness was something to despise, pinching and punching my belly, thighs, and chest—parts of my body larger and less masculine than other middle school boys.

My short choco-chunky ass looked like Latarian in that news clip that went viral back in '08.

Sometimes I noticed Robbie, a year younger than me, would nod in agreement with those older boys as if he already knew gentle parts amounted to weakness, that thriving as a man of color required trimming one's tenderness.

On occasion, while Robbie mimicked the older boys' taunts about my weight and demeanor, I would notice cars ease alongside the corner, and one of the older boys would lean in through the open passenger-side window, slapping cash into the driver's waiting palm.

I knew what was up, even if I didn't have words for it yet.

Robbie understood, too, and he wanted desperately to take part in whatever economy drove the corner.

No lie, it did look cool, on some Peter Pan's Lost Boys style. Probably seemed better to Robbie than slaving all day in coveralls as a custodian like his dad in D.C. Always working overtime. Never around.

Robbie and I knew better than to aspire to sell drugs on a quiet intersection. But like Latarian suggests in the WPBF 25 news segment that made him famous, doing what we should doesn't always hold the same pleasure as doing what we shouldn't.

Guess Robbie also thought like Latarian. "It's fun to do bad things."

But there has to exist more to this shared ideology than thrill seeking. Robbie and Latarian aren't just caricatures.

I remember Robbie leading me to a rust-spotted, sun-faded, yellow trailer home. He knocked twice before pushing through the front door. It took a few seconds for my eyes to adjust to the dim inside. The blinds were closed over every window, and dark wood wall paneling and shaggy maroon carpet swallowed the thin beams of light sneaking through the plastic slats.

I smelled rot, mold, the musk of weed, and stale malt liquor. Robbie pulled me deeper into the space. The floor sloped to the center of a living room. The support beams squealed and bounced under my weight.

Reminded me of moving on a boat. Feared I might sink through.

On a loveseat, two blue figures shared a cigarette. Both of them wore fitted sport caps. One leaned forward to speak. The voice, grim and feminine, cursed Robbie for barging into the house. She warned him. She could have shot us.

Robbie introduced her as his aunt Tits.

"Tits," I repeated, nodding in acknowledgment, resisting a smile.

Tits had on a basketball jersey and the muscles in her bare arms, speckled with tattoos, visibly constricted when she moved. "This is my girl," Tits said, tendons tightening up through her neck to tilt her head to the person next to her on the couch. Tits snatched the cigarette from her partner's mouth and inhaled it. For a moment the burning ember lit Tits' eyes, shrouded beneath the brim of her hat.

Saw a slash cutting through her eyebrows. Looked like she'd been cut up once or twice.

Tits' girl stood and walked to the kitchen adjoining the living room and fumbled through the cabinet below the sink. Tits asked Robbie about his grandmother and then inquired about my mom. I stammered about calling home earlier that day.

Tits' girl returned with an innocuous backpack. She stood still for a moment, considering Robbie before handing the book bag to me. The weight felt comparable to a ream of printing paper from my mom's office at Bell Atlantic.

Tits told us to run the bag north to Lincoln Village. She gave us the street name of one of the boys known to lurk around the corners.

She issued a few simple rules: "Don't open the pack. Don't stop to talk to anybody. Stay cool if you see police. And, if anything happens to the bag, keep riding forever because if I ever catch up with y'all, I'll murder you."

Tits didn't give a euphemism. The two syllables, Mur-Der,

bam, *boom*, bellowed in the darkness. Tits waved Robbie and me out without another comment.

Outside I slipped my arms through the straps of the backpack. Robbie picked his bike up off the ground and I did the same. Over a decade later, I'd go online to map the distance of our delivery to Lincoln Village. 1.1 kilometers. 0.7 miles. Straight on Sixth Street, left on Washington Street, a right onto Eighth Street, and a final turn into a subsidized housing complex. Approximately three minutes, but the distance traveled that day breaks out of time in my memory, scrambled in the heat of summer and fear.

Operating on a kind of instinct, Robbie and I rode in silence. He pedaled in front and I remained a car-length behind. The contents of the book bag slapped my sweating back in rhythm with the rise and push of my legs.

A whole mess of stuff was running though my head: Curiosity about whether the bag carried weapons or drugs or cash, questions about what other people might do to get what I had in my possession, visions of where law enforcement officers might be hiding along the route, ready to arrest me.

While I was daydreaming about escaping the police on

my bike, Robbie started slowing down. I followed him into the parking lot of Lincoln Village, a horseshoe of narrow two-story apartments resembling row houses.

Robbie and I spotted the older boy Tits had named. He stood out in a red shirt—looking like that poet I'd see at the lit conference twenty-something years later. Robbie and I rode up to the corner boy, and he seemed to have been expecting us because he walked us both into one of the apartments. Inside half a dozen brothers lounging, smoking, and drinking. An older boy from one of the corners reached for the backpack, and I passed it to him. Everyone in the room looked at me with new respect. They praised me and Robbie on a job well done, and another homie gave each of us a twenty.

I can't deny beaming, climbing down those stairs onto the street.

I wished some of the hood kids that laughed at me in school could glimpse me leaving a trap spot.

Robbie suggested we head to the gas station to buy some snacks. On the bike ride over, Robbie prattled about *street credibility* and *legitimacy*. He reflected on the ease it took to make twenty dollars in less than an hour. More than his father makes at work, probably more than my mom made at her job. He said he would return to Tits again soon and welcomed me to join him. This had been a test, and now he assured me that we could both make regular deliveries.

We reached the gas station on Fifth Street and parked our bikes.

Followed Robbie as he strutted past the cashier. Picked up sodas and sunflower seeds. Robbie offered to pay since more money was sure to come.

The gas station attendant scowled. He asked where Robbie had acquired a twenty-dollar bill.

Robbie responded, "I got it from your momma last night."

The cashier closed the register, handed Robbie back his banknote, and told us both to get out. Robbie stormed to the exit, cursing the man and *threatening to involve some roughnecks from the Southside.*

Outside the gas station, Robbie couldn't stop grinning. The shit that day had excited him. I pulled each of my fingers, cracking knuckles like I always do. Nervous.

Robbie asked me what I wanted to do next, and I told him I was hungry and tired. I said I wanted to return to my grandmother's house for lunch.

Robbie teased me about always being hungry. He suggested we both go back to the corners.

I told him, "Kinda getting tired of all that."

He sucked his teeth, shook his head, and said, "Whatever."

Dismissing me, Robbie hopped on his bicycle.

He didn't bother saying goodbye. He disappeared.

I rode off, too, in a different direction.

Didn't hang with cuz the next day when he came round to the house. Gave him some excuse about feeling sick or something. I didn't spend time with Robbie again. I saved the twenty in my wallet, where it stayed for months. After that, I don't know the details of Robbie's life. *Last I heard*, years later, *Robbie's pop told my mom that Robbie got kicked out of high school for some hood shit, dealing and stealing.* Now, I don't often think of Robbie unless prompted, like in the instance I see a prominent African American literary scholar *in a tight-ass T-shirt* propagating an idea that appears lighthearted but carries deeper implications.

Is the poet in the tee aware of what happened to Latarian Milton after the height of internet celebrity, after Latarian made prime-time cable television appearances, after a popular late-night animated series satirized the seven-year-old for stealing his grandmother's Dodge Durango, hitting four cars, running over two mailboxes, and then crashing into a curb, sideswiping a realty sign? Does the poet know two weeks after Latarian became a viral meme and ushered in a new expression of Objectivism, Latarian beat his grandmother inside of a Walmart because she refused to purchase fried chicken?

After public fascination with Latarian Milton dwindled, he appeared to change. WPBF 25 interviewed Latarian again in 2015 as he graduated middle school. He seemed well—"on the right track," the reporter said—a model for how young men of a certain race can reinvent themselves. However, three years later, police arrested Latarian for the armed robbery and carjacking of a Lyft driver. *When cops came for lil cuz Latarian, he removed the stolen car keys from his pocket and threw them on the ground... Bruh.* Like Robbie, Latarian might have followed the principles shared by older boys lost on a corner.

To those born into the fallout of centuries of subservience to a nation that has consistently attempted to erase them, Latarian's words echo an inherent desire to be known and seen, to live free without apology or obligation to anyone, the freedom to choose a life driven by one's own sense of purpose.

Maybe the poet at the literary conference wears Milton's

words ironically, to convey the absurdity some folks face when the pursuit of their own individual gratification and wellbeing is always weighed against the rise and fall of an entire population.

For Latarian, Robbie, the poet, *and me*, whether we learn to thrive by conforming to a society not designed for us or elevate ourselves by operating beneath that society, we will always serve as examples of others who look like us. When the challenges of our environment evoke a survival response, we must also contend with the knowledge that our choices could contribute to those same problems for someone who shares a resemblance.

This pressure can fracture and compartmentalize identity, *get you feeling like you're two different people.* Maybe this irks me.

Thinking about the academic in the bloodshot tee, I'm reminded how little separates my flesh and spirit from Robbie or Latarian. *Didn't share these thoughts with the poet or speak on his clothing.* Or ask if proceeds from the sale of the shirt might go to Latarian's bail and legal fees.

Exchanging nods, acknowledging each other's movement through a predominantly white space, I only wished for the poet what I'd want for myself.

Maybe dude wore the shirt because it's funny in a way, a mad joke.

35.

After August 2014, I began obsessing over the Missouri Compromise of 1820. I read it again and again, marveling at how well the document conveys the intention of its creators, their lasting influence for a US territory.

I've often assigned the Compromise in my English Composition courses as part of an exercise in rhetorical analysis. Students read the Compromise individually for homework. When they come to class, I divide the learners into groups of three or four. Each group is assigned two sections of the document; they then have a set amount of time to summarize the legislation of the sections in contemporary language—"How would you explain what each section enacts in a social media post?" I move around the room while they work, monitoring and answering questions, guiding them to pay special attention to some of the most notable elements.

Like how Section 3 grants voting rights only to free white males over twenty-one.

And Section 6.5 decrees that land in the territory will be reserved for the president of the United States, land will be reserved for a seminary of learning, the sale of land sold by the government will be tax exempt...later complicated by the Morrill Act of 1862, which granted federally controlled land to states to sell and raise funds to endow educational institutions.

And Section 8 officially establishes Missouri as a slave state, and reinforces that fugitive slaves in other states can be lawfully claimed and returned.

After the students finish sharing their summaries, I usually distribute or display images of riots in Ferguson, Missouri, following the murder of Michael Brown. I discuss the 2017 travel advisory issued for the state of Missouri by the National Association for the Advancement of Colored People (NAACP). I ask the learners to consider how elements of the Missouri Compromise of 1820 might contextualize the photographs of anguished faces, streets illuminated by car fires, police pointing automatic rifles at unarmed civilians, and the NAACP's decision to label Missouri as a territory to fear.

The students and I talk about the lasting effects of regulation that originally defined the region's citizenship by gender, race, and class; how the appropriation of land inhabited by indigenous people built the wealth of institutions that for so long reinforced the advancement of men who most closely resembled the authors of the Compromise. Together, my students and I consider how rhetoric used to establish a territory two hundred years ago might continue to shape, order, and divide a population today.

36

"I would look at her and think to myself about social forces and the pressures massing and poised, waiting to attack us."

37.

Every day, limit the amount of time spent in public. While outside, walk fast and try to stay mindful to keep hands visible, out of pockets, even in the cold.

[38.]

"I conceive there is more barbarity in eating a man alive, than when he is dead; in tearing a body limb from limb by racks and torments, that is yet in perfect sense; in roasting it by degrees; in causing it to be bitten and worried by dogs and swine (as we have not only read, but lately seen, not amongst inveterate and mortal enemies, but among neighbors and fellow-citizens, and, which is worse, under color of piety and religion), than to roast and eat him after he is dead."

39. DEATH OF A MISER

For Hieronymus Bosch

I know death. Death stalks, waiting for invitation, dressed as something familiar. Death creeps in peripheral sight, not in flowing robes but as hereditary illness, disease, legacies of violence and oppression.

There is no art to dying slow.

Death pervades, persistent and rarely artful. To inhabit a certain space, a certain skin, means to know death more intimately; to court one's own end, consistently screaming into silence, "Not now!"

Not if.

Not never.

Just please...

not now.

Not...

Like...

This.

I failed to save my grandma from death. Like so many living in poverty, preventable circumstances killed her. My mother, although considered middle class, met similar conditions: diabetes, hypertension, stroke, hemorrhage, abrasions, wounds and their infection. My savings were depleted. Credit cards maxed. I began throwing collection letters from hospitals into the trash. I stopped answering my phone to avoid speaking to debt agencies.

I could no longer afford to keep my mother alive.

So I removed my dead grandmother's revolver from the drawer of my nightstand.

I carried the gun into my mother's bedroom beside mine.

While mom slept and writhed in pain, I wept over her softly.

I didn't wake her.

Feelings of uselessness subsided with the weight of the snub-nose revolver in my hand. The hopelessness dissipated with the movement of pulling back the cylinder release to unload all the bullets but one.

And then I saw death as an intruder, standing in the doorway of my mother's bedroom. Wrenching back the hammer, I fired wildly at the apparition. But no blasts accompanied the clicks from the weapon.

As death inched closer, my mind fell silent.

I pressed the barrel of the gun to my temple and pulled the trigger.

The violent shake of the hammer connecting with the firing pin startled me, and my thoughts returned.

Death vanished.

The sole bullet remained in the chamber.

My mother snorted awake.

x

I sometimes think accumulating wealth would ease my passing and salve the suffering before death. I think I might like to join those who die comfortably among their riches, like pharaohs and royals. In my baser moments, I too aspire to celebrity and nobility, to get rich or die trying.

Because if cash rules everything around me, why couldn't wealth intercede between my life and my death?

I started saving, adopted schemes suggested by financial gurus and fiscally responsible friends, purchased stocks, lived cheaply, looked into CD accounts and a Roth IRA, set aside money every week, every month, every year. But the threat of death and exorbitant medical expenses leveled my net worth. Leveled me. How do I insulate myself, and those I'd die for, against a cold fatality? The persistence of the myth that perseverance and hard work are enough doesn't make it true.

I sensed "intergenerational earnings elasticity" long before I knew its name. Friends at school would mention inheritances and trust funds or gripe about how little they received in their grandparents' wills. I noticed all of these friends had a different skin color than mine. Many of these friends had heirlooms, priceless trinkets they could bring in for show-and-tell, antiques they could trace along with their lineage to countries in Europe. They all knew where their families began. I knew some of my own heritage because my father emigrated from West Africa. My friends often punctuated their familial tales with details about their ancestors' poverty, how much their forefathers struggled to build prosperity in a new world. Despite whatever stereotypes were associated with their genealogy, whatever persecution their family faced, my friends' ancestors had managed to thrive. Sometimes their stories caused me to flush with shame. In a country built on immigrant narratives, I'm not sure anyone can resist engaging in a kind of comparative suffering.

Why hadn't my ancestors done a better job pulling themselves up out of scarcity? Why couldn't they leave me something valuable and measurable? Now, as an adult, I recognize the many aspects of society designed to prevent upward mobility and the challenges presented at birth for paying wealth forward to the next generation. I identify more with those accustomed to getting snapped back like a rubber band, segments of the population for whom the elastic is pulled too tight.

I understand an inclination toward nefariousness in order to improve one's quality of life. I don't condone the subjugation of others, violence, stealing, or breaking. I do not approve of crimes against others as a response to the fear of death. But I understand.

x

What does it mean to live? Is it to suffer, to thrash against the ideology that wealth is the way to salvation and money is the great equalizer? The ticket to survival?

Hieronymus Bosch believed the temporal anguish of this world is immaterial to the glory revealed to God's faithful after death. In *Death and the Miser*, a triptych panel created around the end of the 15th century, the Dutch painter incorporates common *Ars moriendi* imagery: Christian iconography of conflicts between good and evil, creeping demons, pleading angels, crucifixes, and personifications of death brandishing arrows. The painting urges the viewer to ignore the pain of all that conspires to do them harm, resist worldly temptations, give up the pursuit of wealth, and to die well.

This sounds noble.

But when faced with the prospect of living and dying on my knees—an existence broke and tired leading to an unlawful end, weary and broken—it is difficult not to despair, not to lose patience, difficult not to resort to pride and greed. With death lurking over me, I found it very difficult to ignore the connections between wealth and living, between scarcity and dying.

When my mother lost the ability to walk, and hoisting her from the bed to the wheelchair threatened to tear my back, and the physicians at the dialysis center rushed her to the hospital, and she spent weeks in and out of intensive care units, and the medical center discharged her to a long-term rehabilitation facility, and a government tax penalty obstructed federal financial assistance for the daily health expenses, and I had to leave to avoid eviction from the costly ADA accessible apartment I had rented, and sell and whittle my possessions, when I was homeless and helpless, broke and navigating a divorce, death appeared to me again.

Dressed in the leftover bottles of my mother's oxycodone, I swallowed palms of death seeing no way to buy myself out of the pain of living.

x

I have five tattoos, each a reminder of an instance in which I failed to end my own life. Left leg, a Chinese character, *dào*, meaning the way, a path forward; above the Mandarin, a Bible verse citation, Romans 8:13–39, a scripture my grandmother gave to me years before she passed; left triceps, a Celtic cross composed of interlocking lines and curves like tendon; right forearm, an Edison bulb with a number two pencil as its filament. These patches of cheap, fading ink signify moments when the fear of living appeared too great to endure.

I learned to believe in the hierarchies wealth imposes, because this conviction gives stability and order to the uncertainty of life. I've prayed silently to a god of fortune and capital and then grieved in the realization that no amount of money will ever make me safe. My familiarity with death has illustrated that no amount of wealth can ever fully guarantee that I won't be killed by one of the many problems that target the populations I'm bound to.

When I last confronted death, I asked for relief from a higher power. I couldn't stop imagining what could be done for me with the money tithed to gold-glittering places of worship. I asked, *God, what can be done for me, right here and now, in a country built and dependent on the division of people into socioeconomic classes; one nation, under God, that has so often employed faith in the crafting of laws that maintain the modes of oppression I face? Lord, could you afford me rest?* I prayed to be saved physically and financially. I pleaded for the kind of wealth Bosch would implore me not to covet.

In the effort to accrue money, it is easy to miss the light from others, promising reprieve from the shadows.

The answer to my yearning for greater wealth came from the communities around me. I found salvation in the generosity of friends, the comfort of family, and the compassion of strangers. They continue to teach me to have faith in the ability of humans to ease suffering and enrich the lives of one another. I received food and shelter and work and charity, enough to do more than just survive.

Words my mother gave me in my youth have echoed in the actions of others. She said, "Baby, living is something we do together."

My last tattoo rests on my left wrist: a pilcrow, commonly known as a paragraph symbol, a piece of punctuation used to denote a split from old *capitula* and branching forward faithfully into new passages, the start of another section.

40.

Every day, bend and bow, and remember to smile even when the blood begins to boil.

41.

Heard 'em brand brothers I knew, called them animals, brutes.

Better to be wild souls than those who'd cage a nation.

[42.]

"...And when it hit me, I had my hands in the air. And I'm thinking I just got shot! And I'm saying, 'Sir, why did you shoot me?' And his words to me were, 'I don't know.'"

43.

Every day, learn new words for terror. Every day, without rest.

44. THE CITY VS. MLK

For Dawn & Matt Hicks

Maybe it was a lie by omission, my response when the judge inquired into my history. Standing for jury selection in the city's case against Montez Lamont King, I denied having any relationship with the prosecution that might affect my objectivity. But when asked to divulge connections with the arresting officer, any history, I avoided glancing over at Lieutenant Horton, who sat on the witness stand.

If Lieutenant Horton remembered me from the ride-along we shared many months earlier, she didn't betray any signs of recognition. She looked perfectly composed with her hair pulled back into a tight bun and her uniform so neatly pressed and fitted that it lent her the authority of someone with a higher rank, like a chief or even a general. But she remained polite and respectful of the central power in the room, and every response to the judge was followed by a quick and courteous "Your Honor."

I've always wanted to embody that same composure, not just in the courtroom but every day I move through the world.

I've always been attracted to a life in uniform, always admired the idea of being seen and regarded as someone heroic. Not like a superhero, although that is another fantasy. I guess what I mean is I've always wanted to be someone whose self-sacrifice would be honored and remembered.

And all I'm saying is maybe this predilection toward meaningful sacrifice and the desire to demonstrate what some might consider duty is why when asked by the judge if I had any history that might impact my ability to give a fair determination, I could feel my posture begin to mirror Lieutenant Horton, my back straightening, jaw tightening, as I looked solemnly at the head of the court and said, "No, Your Honor."

x

Weeks prior to her detention of Lamont King during a routine traffic stop, I accompanied the lieutenant on a ride-along. I observed Horton respond to three incidents over Halloween weekend. The first, a domestic disturbance between two drunk lovers.

We arrived in the cop car to find an African American woman wearing a holey navy sleeping gown, a burgundy fleece pullover, and lime bedroom slippers. She stood waiting for us in the street in front of a weather-stripped shotgun home, sloping on its sinking foundation.

"Wait here," Horton said. "Don't get out no matter what."

She and I had only just started the evening together. I had met her at the police station, and we had fumbled and smiled through awkward pleasantries and politeness common between two people not entirely sure about the other's motivations. While I'm sure she was suspicious of me, as a writer of color and former local journalist asking to accompany a police officer patrol, she didn't ask me what prompted me to do a ride-along. And I didn't ask what would lead her to volunteer to share her work with me. When I first discovered I'd be paired with Horton, a woman, I felt a sense of relief. I knew I'd feel more comfortable around her than a male officer, especially a white male officer. I accepted that my comfort around Horton involved underlying misogyny and the fact that, at three hundred pounds and five feet, ten inches, I could overpower Horton, a head shorter and less than half my weight. At the time, I didn't think about the ways my size, gender, and race might have also made her feel less comfortable.

So, when she told me not to leave the car as she prepared

to respond to a potentially violent situation, I experienced a surge of protectiveness and guilt out of a dereliction of chivalry. I fought the urge to go with her, nodding to show I understood her authority. I became hyperaware of the straps of the seatbelt binding me to the passenger seat of her police cruiser. She slammed her door and approached the woman standing in the road. Dusk was beginning to settle in, and above the trees lining the street, a full moon was becoming more prominent against gradients of gold and blue.

Officer Horton's voice squawked through the radio mounted to the dashboard—numbers and her current location broadcast to this and other cop cars in the area. Alone in the cruiser, I noted the minimal accessories to Horton's car. On a handle that jutted through the driver's door to operate the searchlight mounted above the side mirror, Horton had hung three additional pairs of handcuffs. The stark reality that there might be a need for the cuffs clashed with the only accent of color in the car, a glittering butterfly-shaped hair barrette clasped to the sun visor above my head. Bedazzled with sparkling rainbow gems, the large clip could keep Horton's thick, dark hair pulled back tightly. I wondered what Horton was like out of uniform. I tried to imagine her smile and her laugh, perhaps something low, like a series of coughs, or maybe she snorts when she finds something really funny.

Then I caught the clack-pop of a screen door and the flash of a human body bursting out of the house. The woman, shouting and stumbling barefoot, barreled at Horton and the civilian in the street. I bolted upright in my seat.

Horton held up a flat palm in front of her, and the belligerent lady halted a few feet away, still screaming at the woman in fluffy lime slides. Her ashen dreads shook as she yelled. The grey ropes sprouting from her head matched the patches of dry scales covering the skin of her arms and legs revealed by her too-short muumuu dress. I guessed that she was the reason we had been called there. The pair might have been in their fifties, or perhaps much younger and aged by poverty. Horton watched the two of them argue for a couple of minutes. Horton rested her hands on her waist, just above her utility belt, her fingers inches above her Taser and gun. Eventually, Horton raised her hand again and calmed them. As she spoke, I could see the shoulders of the civilians slowly drop, and the taut cords of their necks relax. The women nodded at each other, looking upset but somewhat in agreement. They turned away from Horton and returned to the house grumbling to each other, content enough with the threatening peace

Horton had brought between them. Once they returned inside their property, Horton turned to the cruiser.

I waited for Horton to settle into the driver's seat to call some words and numbers over the police radio before asking, "Is everything okay?"

"Oh, yeah," she said. "Just a couple fighting. One got a little too drunk."

She smiled, as if recalling something she didn't share with me. Her lips twisted into a sly half-crescent crashing into her right cheek. She laughed a little, too, a quick, goofy chuckle I never would have imagined.

x

I've been thinking a lot about the history of folks like me supporting ruling powers at home and abroad. Oftentimes this support came at the expense of other people of color, like the 10th Cavalry Regiment of the United States Army. Dubbed Buffalo Soldiers, the 10th Cavalry comprised African Americans. They served in the American Indian Wars from 1866 to the end of the nineteenth century, helping the US government's violent expansion through the Great Plains and the Southwest.

On May 7, 1915, a German U-boat torpedoed a British steamship and prompted America's involvement in World War I. Soon, the US Congress passed the Selective Service Act, initiating a draft requiring *all* young men, regardless of race, to register for military service. The decision to include African Americans in the draft was largely based on former President Theodore Roosevelt's positive experience leading Buffalo Soldiers into battle against Native Americans. Roosevelt's opinions swayed then-President Woodrow Wilson, who believed African Americans were too unintelligent and lacked the discipline needed for war. W. E. B. Du Bois was one of many African American leaders and activists who saw the draft as a chance to prove that folks like me deserved racial equality. Hoping the US government would see our loyalty and service to their country, Du Bois encouraged men like me to say, "*first* your Country, *then* your Rights!" Nearly four hundred thousand men like me were registered and inducted into military service and encouraged to show their best devotion to the nation. We should fight hard, demonstrate our ability, and maybe when the war was over, our lives at home in the United States would become fairer and more balanced.

Some of those African American World War I veterans, soldiers of the segregated 371st Infantry Regiment, are buried in the Saint John AME Church cemetery outside of my mother's hometown in Hartsville, South Carolina. I drive by it whenever I visit friends and family in the area. The crumbling headstones share a resemblance to the broken monument constructed by the French in the village of Séchault to honor the men of the 371st Infantry. In pictures I've found on Google, the monument shows damage from shell bombings during World War II. The cracked stone testaments on both sides of the Atlantic are a reminder of failed American social bargains, a broken promise that if we put our country first, our rights as American citizens will be fully honored.

In the seconds before I said, "No, Your Honor," I did not consider that I was following a desire similar to that of many of those Buffalo Soldiers or members of the 371st Infantry: to prove my value through loyalty. I feared losing the chance to perform my civic duty because I saw in it an opportunity to feel like a part of my own nation. Perhaps as a juror I could envision myself as a fuller citizen, as a participant in the legal process—perhaps I could be protected by my country's laws rather than remain a potential casualty of them.

x

Lieutenant Horton and I made circuits around the city, a giant, winding chain of streets linking the edges of gated communities and low-income housing developments. The cruiser crept through one of the HUD apartment blocks, and kids playing in the parking lots froze as Horton and I rolled past. Basketballs slid into storm drains, and kids retreated slowly but steadily off the asphalt and onto the sidewalks and segments of brown grass leading to the shelter of their buildings. I noticed how the kids moved without taking their eyes off the car. Their bodies carried them away while their necks twisted to keep Horton and me in their sight. One little girl tripped over a curb but popped up onto her feet, her eyes on mine as Horton explained how people don't understand half of what officers actually do.

"We aren't trying to be jerks. We're here to protect and serve. Yeah, there are a few bad cops, but it's not all of us." We rode by a group of teenage boys gathered and laughing on the corner of one of the apartment structures. Their joking paused until they were in the rear-view mirrors of the cruiser. "It's not fair, right? For all officers to be judged because of a few. That's what I call prejudice. The majority of us just got into this to help people."

I asked Horton why she decided to be a cop. She told me she used to date an officer. She was in school to become a nurse then. Her boyfriend would often take her on ride-alongs. Horton found she enjoyed the driving, the hours, the workload, and the camaraderie between the officers. "It was fun," she said, and I caught a reflection of my grimace in the passenger-side window. I didn't like the thought of law enforcement being fun.

She asked me why I'd come on a ride-along. I said something about how I thought citizens had a duty to learn as much as they can about their local law enforcement. I said something about community-oriented policing. And then, after several seconds of her silence, I confessed that some part of me has always wanted to protect others and serve the communities I belong to. "In another life," I said, "I might have become a cop or a soldier."

Horton told me I could join the force. The police department is in need of new officers, especially men of color, she said. She told me I could do a lot of good. I could inspire others.

I didn't ask who the others were or what I might inspire in them.

x

In the National Museum of African American History and Culture there hangs a large rag-paper, three-sheet broadside promoting "Men of Color" to enlist in the Union Army. The text, written by Frederick Douglass in 1863, is printed in relief with carved wood type and cast letterpress metal type. In the broadside, Douglass binds the future of men of color to the fate of the nation. He asks freemen to prove their valor and heroism in defense of a United States built on their own oppression. Douglass implores these men to prove they are better than slaves. When thinking about the American Civil War, I often forget there were many instances when men of color were pitted against one another, many fearing that war might be the last opportunity to show that their race was not doomed.

MEN OF COLOR

TO ARMS! TO ARMS!

NOW OR NEVER

This is our golden moment! The Government of the United States calls for every Able-bodied Colored Man to enter the Army for the

Three Years' Service!

And join in Fighting the Battles of Liberty and the Union. A new era is open to us. For generations we have suffered under the horrors of slavery, outrage and wrong; our manhood has been denied, our citizenship blotted out, our souls seared and burned, and our spirits cowed and crushed, and the hopes of the future of our race involved in doubt and darkness. But now our relations to the white race are changed. Now, therefore, is our most precious moment. Let us rush to arms!

FAIL NOW, & OUR RACE IS DOOMED

on this soil of our birth. We must now awake, arise, or be forever fallen. If we value liberty, if we wish to be free in this land, if we love our country, if we love our families, our children, our home, we must strike now while the country calls; we must rise up in the dignity of our manhood, and show by our own right arms that we are worthy to be freemen. Our enemies have made the country believe that we are craven cowards, without soul, without manhood, without the spirit of soldiers. Shall we die with this stigma resting upon our graves? Shall we leave this inheritance of shame to our Children? No! a thousand times NO! We WILL Rise! The alternative is upon us. Let us rather die freemen than live to be slaves. What is life without liberty? We say that we have manhood; now is the time to prove it. A nation or a people that cannot fight may be pitied, but cannot be respected. If we would be regarded men, if we would forever silence the tongue of Calumny, of Prejudice and Hate, let us Rise Now and Fly to Arms! We have seen what Valor and Heroism our Brothers displayed at Port Hudson and Milliken's Bend; though they are just from the galling, poisoning grasp of Slavery, they have startled the World by the most exalted heroism. If they have proved themselves heroes, cannot WE PROVE OURSELVES MEN?

ARE FREEMEN LESS BRAVE THAN SLAVES

More than a Million White Men have left Comfortable Homes and joined the Armies of the Union to save their Country. Cannot we leave ours, and swell the Hosts of the Union, to save our liberties, vindicate our manhood, and deserve well of our Country. MEN OF COLOR! the Englishmen, the Irishmen, the Frenchmen, the German, the American, have been called to assert their claim to freedom and a manly character, by an appeal to the sword. The day that has seen an enslaved race in arms has, in all history, seen their last trial. We are not the only people that opportunity has come. If we are not lower in the scale of humanity than Englishmen, Irishmen, White Americans and other Races, we can show it now. Men of Color, Brothers and Fathers, we appeal to you, by all your concern for yourselves and your liberties, by all your regard for God and humanity, by all your desire for Citizenship and Equality before the law, by all your love for the Country, to stop at no subterfuge, listen to nothing that shall deter you from rallying for the Army. Come Forward, and at once Enroll your Names for the Three Years' Service. Strike now, and you are henceforth and forever Freemen.

E. D. Bassett,	Rev. J. Underdue,	P. J. Armstrong,	Rev. J. C. Gibbs,	Elijah J. Davis,
William D. Forten,	John W. Price,	J. W. Simpson,	Daniel George,	John P. Burr,
Frederick Douglass,	Augustus Dorsey,	Rev. J. B. Trusty,	Robert M. Adger,	Robert Jones,
Wm. Whipper,	Rev. Stephen Smith,	S. Morgan Smith,	Henry M. Cropper,	O. V. Catto,
D. D. Turner,	N. W. Depee,	William E. Gipson,	Rev. J. B. Reeve,	Thos. J. Dorsey,
Jas. McCrummell,	Dr. J. H. Wilson,	Rev. J. Boulden,	Rev. J. A. Williams,	I. D. Cliff,
A. S. Cassey,	J. W. Cassey,	Rev. J. Asher,	Rev. A. L. Stanford,	Jacob C. White,
A. M. Green,	James Needham,	Rev. Elisha Weaver,	Thomas J. Bowers,	Morris Hall,
J. W. Page,	Ebenezer Black,	David B. Bowser,	J. C. White, Jr.,	J. P. Johnson,
L. R. Seymour,	James B. Gordon,	Henry Minton,	Rev. J. P. Campbell,	Franklin Turner,
Rev. William T. Catto,	Samuel Stewart,	Daniel Colley,	Rev. W. J. Alston,	Jesse E. Glasgow,

A Meeting in furtherance of the above named object will be held

And will be Addressed by

U. S. Steam-Power Book and Job Printing Establishment, Ledger Buildings, Third and Chestnut Streets, Philadelphia.

160

In the days leading up to my jury duty in the city's case against Montez Lamont King, I remembered my ride-along with Lt. Horton and responding to a call about an elderly woman experiencing a heart attack in one of the new wealthy communities. By the time we arrived, paramedics had already wheeled the woman into the back of an ambulance. I waited in the car, straining to see signs confirming the woman's breathing. When Horton returned to the car, she was happy to report that the elderly lady was conscious and responding to the EMTs. The woman's daughter, who had dialed 911, would meet the ambulance at the hospital.

We continued on our patrol of the city.

Near a Piggly Wiggly, Horton spotted a silver, rust-spotted town car driving without plates. The vehicle croaked on its poor suspension, the rear of the chassis riding less than a foot from the ground. The rear cabin of the car was packed with yellowing newspaper and discarded fast food containers. I glimpsed the driver: a rail-thin man with cheeks sinking below his thick spectacles and bushy white beard, stark against his tanned skin. Horton spoke to the driver. From the cruiser, I couldn't hear her explain why she was pulling him over, I couldn't hear her questions, but I could hear his heavy barking answers and the anger in his voice. Part of me felt validated to see Horton's right hand hover over the grip of her Taser, the same way she had done when approaching the disagreement between the African American women earlier—standard protocol that didn't change from civilian to civilian.

The driver handed over his license.

Horton returned to the cop car to search the man's identification on the small laptop mounted to the dashboard. She discovered fellow officers had stopped the driver once before for missing plates just hours earlier. I asked Horton what she planned to do. She decided to let him off with a warning. "He looks like he could use a break."

Horton returned the ID to the driver.

I didn't hear a "thank you" in his heavy grumble before he sped away.

Later, I'd try to imagine how this scene would mirror Horton's interaction with Montez Lamont King. Before entering King's driver's license number into the onboard computer in her patrol car, before discovering the warrants out for his arrest for missing court for unpaid parking tickets, would she also consider King deserving of a break?

x

I try to imagine the perspective of the soldiers of the 371st. Imagine being drafted into a war by a nation that kills you. Imagine being told that it is your responsibility to avenge the deaths of over one hundred Americans killed on a British steamship you've never heard of and could have never hoped to ride. Imagine being delayed from deployment to pick that season's cotton harvest because the nation needs you to do that, too. Imagine boarding golden ships to France. Imagine having to abandon the second-rate training you were given because your pale-skinned countrymen refuse to fight alongside you, and adopting the weapons and techniques of foreigners as you enter the fray of battle.

And then, while you trudge east across war-torn countryside that almost looks like home, the thunder of enemy planes rips through grey clouds overhead, and a message rains down on coarse paper.

COLOURED SOLDIERS
OF THE STATES!

They told you at home that the Germans kill their prisoners. Well, that's

LIE Nr. 1

and it's about the biggest lie ever invented. How in the name of common sense can you believe it, Boys?

There are about **three million prisoners of war** in Germany now! They ain't dead ones either! You can bet your life they're mighty glad to be out of the trenches and **so are their folks at home.**

— □□□ —

They told you that the prisoners are being illtreated by the Germans. That's

LIE Nr. 2

but it's a darned good second! There **never** was any illtreatment of prisoners, neither in the German lines nor in the camps, **and that's a fact!**

You'd soon be wise about it, should **you** be taken prisoner! You'd be sent to a camp in

Southern Germany.

Why Southern? Because the climate is milder down there. You'd find a job of the kind you like and you'd be **paid** for your work.

— □□□ —

They told you at home that the Germans are starving their prisoners, didn't they? That's

LIE Nr. 3

and it ain't a very clever one. You'll find enough to eat over here and a nicely heated room too! Don't you worry, boys! You would'nt have to live in a damp hole as you do now! When the war is over you'd return to your folks **alive** and that certainly is worth something! Ain't it? Don't let yourself be bluffed into death, boys! You are risking **your own skin** all the time! Don't forget, that you've but one **life to loose** and **that's a very precious one!**

Following World War I, African American soldiers returned home to the advancement of Jim Crow laws that furthered institutionalized economic, social, and educational divides. Du Bois changed his mind about putting country before individual rights. In the August 1919 issue of his magazine *The Crisis*, he wrote, "They cheat us and mock us; they kill and slay us; they deride our misery. When we plead for the naked protection of the law, there where a million of our fellows dwell, they tell us to 'GO TO HELL!' TO YOUR TENTS, O ISRAEL! And FIGHT, FIGHT, FIGHT for Freedom."

x

I asked Horton to drop me off downtown. She offered to drop me off at my home, but I declined the courtesy; some instinctual part of me felt uncomfortable with her knowing where I lived. I thanked her for sharing her world with me and for being so open and honest. Horton thanked me for my interest and for taking the time to get to know what officers really do. Sliding out of the cop car, we didn't shake hands, but I paused and so did she. We stared at each other, smiling awkwardly, searching the silence between us for a gesture that might convey the significance of our time together. In that pause, we didn't hug; no fist bumps or daps. In those last seconds, we didn't drop our courtesy. Neither of us mentioned Tulsa police officer Betty Shelby or her acquittal a month earlier on charges of first-degree manslaughter in the murder of Terence Crutcher, a forty-year-old motorist, not "a bad dude," just an unarmed man with car trouble, looking for help with his vehicle stuck in the middle of the street. He was looking for help from Shelby, and instead she shot him to death. He was slain by her imagination. Horton and I didn't talk about that in those last moments together. Instead, we settled on exchanging polite smiles and a nod of acknowledgment—*I see you*, our bodies said.

Horton and I did not share this gesture months later at the jury selection or after that when Montez Lamont King didn't appear for his day in court, and I was relieved of my duty to have to decide his innocence or guilt. I avoided direct eye contact with Horton; I can't be sure if she did the same. Her focus seemed to alternate between the prosecutor and the judge. Montez Lamont King's bail was forfeited and another warrant issued for his arrest. I felt a sense of concern for King, a person I never got a chance to see in person. During the days following the trial date, I thought of the many factors that could obstruct an African American male from receiving a fair trial. Maybe I thought I could have tipped those scales. Maybe part of me wanted to ensure that Montez Lamont King faced a jury of his peers or, at least, a jury with someone who might be more experienced with the systems of prejudice that might have contributed to his delinquency. Maybe the omission of my familiarity with Horton wasn't just another example of an African American man agreeing to put the lawfulness of his country before the rights of his race.

x

I never saw Lt. Horton again. I wished to find her years later when Amber Guyger, tired and overworked, ignored thousands of details indicating she had entered the wrong apartment, not her own, and shot and killed Botham Shem Jean, a twenty-six-year-old accountant who resembled me in pictures when he smiled. It happened in Dallas, the same city where Micah Xavier Johnson—an African American and an Afghan War veteran driven mad by the number of police shootings of men who look like him—shot and killed five police officers and injured nine others.

I wanted to find Horton again when a jury convicted Guyger

to a ten-year murder sentence. I wanted Horton to tell me she'd never be as careless as Amber Guyger or Betty Shelby or any of those other cops some would try to explain away as a rare bad apple. I wanted to talk with Horton again and have her swear that my willingness to serve might counter some learned fears about citizens like me.

"Because how does one memorialize the everyday? How does one, in the words so often used by such institutions, 'come to terms with' (which usually means move past) ongoing and quotidian atrocity?"

I'm still listening to the fourth record from Run the Jewels, the rap duo comprising El-P and Killer Mike. The album (*RTJ4*) was released during the height of the Black Lives Matter demonstrations held in over two thousand cities and towns throughout all fifty American states and in communities around the globe. The protests followed the murder of George Floyd by a Minneapolis police officer on May 25; the killing of Dreasjon "Sean" Reed in Indianapolis by police on May 6; the death of Breonna Taylor, killed by Louisville police in Kentucky in her own apartment on March 13; and the death of Ahmaud Arbery, shot by a former Georgia police officer on February 23.

I'm averse to using the word "timely" to describe the arrival of *RTJ4*; that word is so often used to promote art by people of color while also presenting their work on injustice as something like a fad. Timely isn't the word to express how much *RTJ4* speaks to the cultural and political moment in which it appeared, or how it expresses the culmination and continuation of systems of oppression. One song in particular stood out to me on the first listen: "walking in the snow." I recognized many of my thoughts and emotions in Killer Mike's verses:

And every day on the evening news they feed you fear for free

And you so numb you watch the cops choke out a man like me

Until my voice goes from a shriek to whisper, "I can't breathe"

And you sit there in house on couch and watch it on TV

The most you give's a Twitter rant and call it a tragedy

But truly the travesty, you've been robbed of your empathy

Replaced it with apathy, I wish I could magically

Fast forward the future so then you can face it

And see how fucked up it'll be

The lyrics were on repeat in my headphones for days as I followed hashtags like #PublishingPaidMe and #BlackInTheIvory that demonstrated how difficult it is for a person of color to move through white institutions. Killer Mike's voice played and echoed between my ears on a quiet walk shortly after my mother called to tell me about the fatal shooting of Rayshard Brooks in Atlanta on June 12. I heard the music as I reflected on how nearly one quarter of the lives lost in fatal police shootings each year are Black, and how maddening this statistic is when one considers that Black people make up less than fourteen percent of the US population. "walking in the snow," and especially the aforementioned lyrics, speak to many of my fears as a Black man, and my frustration with the prevalence of empty rhetoric and useless platitudes whenever tragedies force the general public to notice systemic racism.

I saw hundreds of statements from organizations announcing their recommitment to diversity and allyship in the publishing industry and academia—the institutions by which I struggle to financially support myself and my family. "walking in the snow" stayed on repeat as I scrolled through hundreds of black boxes on Instagram, hundreds of *listening-and-learnings* and social media rants about equality. I cued the song when Ugandan writer Hope Wabuke posted screenshots on Twitter of a private email exchange between her fellow board members at the National Book Critics Circle. The post showed that other board members had objected to releasing a racial equality statement that mentioned the fact that white gatekeepers have continually stifled Black voices. In one leaked email, a member wrote, "I've seen far more of white people helping Black writers than of Black people helping white writers." Perhaps he hadn't listened hard enough to testimonies from Black authors and scholars. While reading Wabuke's response to questions about her resignation, I heard the *RTJ4* refrain, "Just got done walking in the snow / Goddamn that motherfucker cold." Wabuke said, "It is not possible to change these organizations from within, and the backlash will be too dangerous for me to remain."

Part of me knows it is impossible for me to change academia or publishing, that my teaching and writing will never overturn the oppressive foundations on which these institutions rest. But even if I can't do it alone, I hope that with the peers and allies that I find in the blizzard we can find new, warmer ways to educate and publish that aren't predicated on racism.

I think of the song now whenever I think about the ways institutions that benefit from sharing Black stories so often reinforce white supremacy. I conjure the image of walking through snow as I continue pushing and trudging through blankets of whiteness. And it's cold. And it's dangerous for me to keep walking—it might kill me—but I try to warm myself with the belief that in all this whiteness my shape may make some kind of shelter for others.

"I seek a way to bring all my feelings and thoughts together to create un testimonio that's harmonious, cohesive, and healing. Only by speaking of these events and by creating do I become visible to myself and come to terms with what happens."

48. FOLKLORE

You know the story of Little Eight John? The one about a boy who looks fine but doesn't act fine—*as mean as mean there was*, or so it goes. The kid, Little Eight John, keeps breaking the rules. His mom tells him not to kick frogs or bad luck will come to the family. The boy does it anyway, kicks a fat bunch of toads and the very next morning the family's cow stops producing milk and Little Eight John's baby sister gets colic.

His mother tells him not to sit in chairs backward. She says it'll bring the family trouble. Of course, Little Eight John immediately takes a seat in reverse and the damn cornbread burns in the oven and the butter doesn't churn. So this goes on. His mom tells Little Eight John not to climb trees in his church clothes, not to count his teeth, not to sleep with his head at the foot of the bed. He does it all anyway, and the farm's potatoes don't grow; his mother gets an incurable case of hiccups; his baby sister gets whooping cough; the family goes broke. Finally, Little Eight John's mom tells him not to complain about going to church on Sunday. Little Eight John, being who he is, starts moaning on Sunday morning. His mother warns him; she says his behavior will conjure a water demon called Old Raw Head Bloody Bones.

You know how this ends. Old Raw Head Bloody Bones comes into the house that very night, storms into the family dinner, and reduces Little Eight John to a spot of goo on the dining table. The mother grabs a rag. She calmly wipes the spot that was Little Eight John.

Viewed one way, it is a simple tale about why we need to listen to our parents. Viewed another way, it's a story reflecting a common anxiety among African American families. Little Eight John isn't doing anything particularly bad. Little Eight John is only guilty of not being an exceptional child. He laughs in defiance of his mother's warnings, but the narrative never encourages the receiver to consider that Little Eight John is not acting out maliciously. The kid might not know any better. He never gets an opportunity to grow up, make mistakes, do better, become a man.

To me, this is a story about a cultural insistence on a Black child being good, transcendent even, because his bad behavior might bring negative consequences to his kith and kin. Little Eight John's narrative teaches young African American men that their bad behavior can threaten the universal survival of their families; there is no redemption, only sacrifice, their wiping away.

49.

I heard them call me criminal, some *thing* or *other*.

I heard them call me _____, something or other.

50. NOVEMBER 2020

On Election Day, I woke around 4 a.m. I made some tea and toast, grabbed my voter registration card, wallet, a cap, and a facemask. I prepared myself to encounter voter suppression. I imagined having to walk past armed Trump Army poll-watchers who might look at the color of my skin and try to intimidate me. I got to my polling place, a Lutheran church, around 5:30. I was surprised by the absence of Make America Great Again hats. I was surprised to see so many young people, college kids shuffling in their sweats and leggings against the early morning chill. I even spotted one of my former students.

I can't recall ever being so eager to stand in line.

While waiting to vote I read *Memoirs of a Polar Bear* by Yoko Tawada on my e-reader. I highlighted the following quote with my thumbs: "And if we don't get this not-very-much exactly right, we will not survive." I read it over and over again. I thought about it when my turn came to take a ballot. I didn't cast my vote until close to 7 a.m. By then, the line of voters had begun wrapping around the church. On the drive home I listened to the song "America" from the 1961 *West Side Story* motion picture soundtrack. A hopeful smile spread across my face as Rita Moreno sang, *Life can be bright in America*.

x

In 2016, I published a personal essay collection called *Harbors*. It was about a lot of things but mostly it was about—as Du Bois puts it—how it feels to be a problem. Since Trump's inauguration in 2017, I've realized I'm trying to answer how it feels to be *told* that I am a problem. What does it mean to be reminded daily through national rhetoric, institutional regulation, and public demonstrations that large segments of this population don't want me in America and don't know what to do with the fact that I am?

On Election Day, after I returned home from voting, I took my dog out into the front yard. A large pickup truck with a pole for a flag depicting Trump as Rambo drove past twice, the driver staring at me behind his sunglasses. The same truck returned later that day, passing my house at a crawl with a dozen other vehicles sporting Trump flags and blaring car horns. Peering through my blinds at the parade, I remembered the lyrics from *West Side Story*:

Life is all right in America (If you're all-white in America)

Here you are free and you have pride (Long as you stay on your own side)

The Friday evening after Election Day, I was sulking about the close margins of the voting results. To raise my spirits, my partner recommended I reread *The Carrying: Poems* by Ada Limón. In the piece "A New National Anthem," I felt myself lifted. I raced a highlighter over the line: "like a match being lit / in an endless cave, the song that says my bones / are your bones, and your bones are my bones".

I felt a sense of hope for my country again. That hope was rewarded the next morning during a remote video meeting when one of my colleagues interrupted a point he was making to let us know, "*The Guardian* has just called it!" As my peers vacillated between beaming and bemoaning the fact that Biden was not their most ideal choice, I remembered *West Side Story* and Anita and Bernardo singing on a NYC rooftop. *Life can be bright in America,* I thought to myself, *if we can fight for America.*

x

In the months leading up to November 2020, as hundreds of

thousands gathered publicly, risking their health during a global pandemic to demonstrate their support for racial equality, I was unhopeful that these outpourings would lead to more progressive votes on Election Day. I was happy to be wrong. The world saw a victory against flagrant bigotry; as Biden said in his acceptance speech, it is a bend in the moral universe toward justice. And I believe there could be greater triumphs ahead if we continue to show up for each other. I'm not always sure how to do this, but I think showing up means being seen, heard, and counted, even on days when numbers don't seem to matter as much. It means I keep living and writing—to the next line, paragraph, and page, every day. I continue teaching and inventing new ways to challenge as well as include. These methods are the best I have found to provide myself and others space to redefine what and who we want to be.

I am often tempted to hide and do only what I must to survive. I experience frequent and overt resistance to my attempts to help rear a new kind of nation where its citizens are its purpose and no one is made to feel like a problem. In these moments, I try to remember that the fight to make life all right in America is not a solitary effort, just as the benefits should extended beyond the individual. There are others, toiling beside me, shining a light in an endless cave, sharing their bones.

x

You don't remember climbing the hill out of the forest or how you managed to avoid apprehension. But you do recall praying selfishly for your own rescue.

Now, standing alone in a clearing, watch the treeline.

Wait for blue shadows to emerge from the woods.

When they don't appear, lie on the ground and listen to your heart trying to escape your chest.

The coughing will subside eventually, once your body learns to breathe again.

Later, friends will tell you how fast they saw you run. They'll applaud your remarkable evasion. But you will not escape the feeling of being pursued, the sense that a presence still looms, waiting to shackle you. And you will accept that you must carry this perception all your life.

Embrace this brief respite. Run your sweaty palms over the cool, dry grass. Look to the thin clouds streaked across the sky and smile wider than you have ever smiled.

For now, you are alone at rest.

ACKNOWLEDGMENTS

(1) / "Thieves," *AGNI*; (8) / "March 14, 2002," *Under the Gum Tree*; (11) / "Heathers," *Cherry Tree;* (17) / "Undertow," *Platypus Press*; (25) / "How to Date Me," *AGNI*; (34) / "The Souls of Latarian Milton," *Literary Hub;* (39) / "Death of a Miser," *The Spectacle;* (44) / "The City vs. MLK," *Michigan Quarterly Review;* (46) / *"A Note to the Shareholders," Poets & Writers; (48), Atticus Review.*

With love to Bailey Gaylin Moore and Beckon Palmer LaBrie.

Many thanks to the friends and editors who saw earlier versions of these pieces: Tatiana Ryckman, Nicole Brown, William "Bill" Pearson, Leone Brander, Janna Marlies Maron, Robin Martin, Michelle Tudor, Tina Richardson, Sufiya Abdur-Rahman, David Olimpio, Cheryl Telligman, Robert Long Foreman, Lacey Rowland, Lindsay Fowler, Micaela Bombard, Ashley Andersen, Bailey Boyd, Cassie Donish, Grace Garder, Jacob Hall, Colin Cheney, Reginald Dwayne Betts, Robert Vivian, Said Shaiye, Phong Nguyen, and Anand Prahlad.

I'm very grateful for the continued support from Tim Antonides, Jason Arment, Ron Austin, Gayle Baldwin, Alexa Bartel, Bridgid & Ryan Bender, Al Black, Mike Blair, Conleth Buckley,

Catherine Buni, Mathieu Cailler, Tobias Carroll, Anna Brown, Jennifer Cohen, Lydia Cole, Louise Crowley, Cathleen Cuppett, Jesse Dávila, Mary Catherine Ferrell, Kristie Frederick Daugherty, Tara Dempsey, Celeste Doaks, Madeleine Dubus, Courtney Ford, John Foster, Arlia Frink, Roxane Gay, Andrea S. Gilham, Peter J. Glovanzki, Christina Gustin, Casey Hancock, Jane Poirier Hart, Hopeton Hay, Jennifer Heisel, Dawn & Matthew Hicks, Nick Hilbourn, Greg Hill, Mandy Holland, Adam & Landon Houle, Corinne Jenkinson, Justin Johnson, Kima Jones, Susan King, Karen Kelly, Julia Klimek, Rhoda Knight, Samuel Kolawole, Anu Kumar, Diane Lefer, George Lellis, Nicolas Leon-Ruiz, Sunisa Manning, Jenifer Maritza McCauley, Robert McCready, Josh Michael, Aisha Moorer, Tomás Q. Morin, Damien Miles-Paulson, Mai Nardone, Mel Pennington, John Proctor, Richard Puffer, Victorio Reyes, Mary Rickert, Stephanie Rizzo, Alisa Sass, Elizabeth Schmul, Rion Amilcar Scott, Sophfronia Scott, Sarah Seltzer, James Bernard Short, Javier Starks, Breana Steele, Eli Stewart, Brandon Taylor, John Taylor Stout, Cedric Tillman, Lee Thomas, Isis Thonpson, Rachel Thompson, Erin Record, Laura Reed, Ian Wallace, Michael Waskom, Mac & Mickelle Williams, Talmage Willis, Cheryl Wright-Watkins, Graham Wood, Ben Woodard, Sara Wyatt-Witherspoon,

Kali VanBaale, Natalie M. Zeigler, and C Pam Zhang.

Much love to my family: Dorothy Quist, Hammond J. Quist Jr., Dr. Faustina Quist, Sena Quist, Selorm Quist, Charlie Van Ngo, and Pitchsinee Jiratra-Anant.

With endless gratitude to the organizations that provided me support to do this work: Charles W. and Joan S. Coker Library-Information Technology Center, Vermont College of Fine Arts, Assumption University of Thailand, Kimbilio Fiction, Sundress Academy for the Arts, University of Missouri-Columbia, and the Authors League Fund.

[7] - Terrance Hayes, *American Sonnets for My Past and Future Assassin* (2018).

[10] - Audre Lorde, "Learning from the 60s." (1982).

[13] - UNIDENTIFIED TULSA POLICE OFFICER (September 16, 2016).

[16] - Mammy, *The Birth of a Nation* (1915).

[20] - Langston Hughes, "Empty Houses." *Simple's Uncle Sam* (1965).

22.

Pinderhughes, Elaine B. "African American Marriage in the 20th Century." *Family Process* 41, no. 2 (2002): 269–82.

Choi, Kyung-Hee, Joseph A. Catania, and M. Margaret Dolcini. "Extramarital Sex and HIV Risk Behavior among US Adults: Results from the National AIDS Behavioral Survey." *American Journal of Public Health* 84, no. 12 (1994): 2003–7.

[24] - Saidiya Hartman, *Lose Your Mother: A Journey Along the*

Atlantic Slave Route (2006).

[28] - James Baldwin, "My Dungeon Shook." *The Fire Next Time* (1963).

[30] - Sgt. Stacey Koon (March 1992).

[33] - Chris Rock, *Bring The Pain* (1996).

[36] - James Alan McPherson, "Gold Coast." (1969).

[38] - Michel de Montaigne, "Of Cannibals." (c. 1580).

[42] - Charles Kinsey (July 18, 2016).

[45] - Christina Sharpe, *In the Wake: On Blackness and Being* (2016).

[47] - Gloria E. Anzaldúa, *Light in the Dark / Luz en lo Oscuro: Rewriting Identity, Spirituality, Reality* (2015).

Donald Quist is author of *Harbors*, a Foreword INDIES Bronze Winner and International Book Awards Finalist. He has a linked story collection, *For Other Ghosts*. His writing has appeared in *AGNI*, *North American Review*, *Michigan Quarterly Review*, *The Rumpus*, and was Notable in *Best American Essays* 2018. He is creator of the online nonfiction series PAST TEN. Donald has received fellowships from Sundress Academy for the Arts, Kimbilio Fiction, and served as a Gus T. Ridgel fellow for the English PhD program at University of Missouri.

He is Director of the MFA in Writing at Vermont College of Fine Arts.